CW00386423

FROM BLAND TO BRAND

10 ESSENTIAL BLOCKS TO BUILD YOUR BRAND

JASON FLINTER

THE FLINT
PUBLISHING HOUSE

CONTENTS

A LICK OF PAINT

THE PLAN

What goes in this bit?

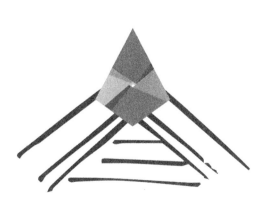

WHAT GOES IN THIS BIT?

I'm sure there are certain conventions I should adhere to when writing a book like this. Maybe acknowledge a few people for inspiring me to type out these ramblings. Get someone you might be familiar with to write me a foreword perhaps. I haven't the faintest idea. It's my first attempt and likely my only one.

From an early age my life has been split into two passionate pursuits; music and branding. This is my first book, but I have written many songs and have recorded and produced several albums for other musicians. My two worlds were magically meshed together when I came across something that the great Gene Simmons, bassist of Kiss, stated;

"Why be in a band when you can be in a **brand**?"

It was something like that!

The front cover is therefore my acknowledgement of these wise words, along with an attempt to bring my two guiding worlds together. I'm also obviously trying to grab your attention whilst having a bit of fun on a photoshoot during a dingy November afternoon.

My editor said it was better than putting the obvious alternative of ten building blocks.

I am writing this first bit last as I've now finished writing the rest of the book, and I can't believe how long it's taken. I have learned a couple of things along the way though.

I'm easily distracted, I'm terrible at spelling and this laptop refuses to admit the word "strapline" exists and keeps putting in "streamline"!

Since I started writing, the world has gone absolutely bonkers (thanks coronavirus) and I had hoped I'd start branching out in my career by giving talks about the topics in this book. That now seems very unlikely and so the online realm beckons.

Actually I had already done a few talks from about 2015 onwards. These slowly evolved my view of this set of ten essential blocks to build a brand.

These thoughts then emerged into a series of videos on my website, which were no more than two or three minutes of information. I was told that "people" switch off after 12 seconds or so online, so don't say too much. On the flip side of that I then got into listening and watching podcasts that lasted two hours or more and so did other "people". The statement that we all had attention spans of a gnat was clearly misleading at best.

It was therefore time to expand on these fleeting videos and put the full flow of my thoughts into this book. Podcasts may come later?

The bigger reason for sharing my thoughts is mainly summarised in the opening chapter, so no need to detail that here.

The other big idea behind this was to cut out the jargon and try to speak as plainly as I could. Over the years I've looked up books, blogs and articles on branding and they have tended to quickly talk about global giants like Apple and Nike (which I admit I will refer to on occasion). It was evident to me that a start-up or SME owner usually found it hard to relate to these businesses in the early days or even years of their new venture. I therefore want these entrepreneurs to understand a branding strategy that they can relate to, and not dismiss that branding is for the companies who already turnover millions, if not billions. They all had to start where you're starting, so I'm hoping this makes branding accessible to you.

Another reason for putting finger to keyboard is that I still have clients who think a brand is simply the logo. This couldn't be further from the truth. It's also a major reason why you won't find a chapter on creating a logo and why it's not one of my ten essential blocks for building a brand. It's probably number 11! I've mentioned it in passing and I've suggested you should have one. There are many other books on the topic.

In the latter part of my professional branding life I've said I "Build BIG brands for small businesses" to really target my primary audience. This book is now an extension of my promise to those start-ups and SMEs and at a considerably reduced rate!!

As a final gift, at the end of each chapter I've asked you three questions so you can immediately start creating your branding strategy. I don't want this to be a flick through and put back on the shelf kind of book. I promise it's not a comprehension test either! If you've just read a chapter with some fresh ideas in your head you might as well put those thoughts down and then you can come back later to embellish.

———

Before you start...

I do have to make it clear that this manuscript has been formatted as best it can thanks to some useful but generic software that converts a Word Doc to an .RTF. I've no idea! This file then gets uploaded to the online platform that you have purchased this book from. With that comes very annoying limitations in layout, sizing, character spacing, leading, typefaces, general gapping, placing of graphics and overall design aesthetic!

So, just before you suggest, 'who the hell am I' to question other people's design decisions, when this very book isn't the best example, then I am in total agreement with you.

I am, however, extremely grateful to Ben Roberts who is helping me 'compile, format and load' in order to get this book published.

That's my excuses over. Let's dive into it.

THE FOUNDATIONS

The six cornerstones of crap
That's mine, get off!
So you think you've got an idea?

THE SIX CORNERSTONES OF CRAP

STOPPING THE DECLINE OF GOOD DESIGN

1 - Who cares?

When I left university (or "Poly" as it was way back in the 80s) I was armed with a scalpel, a Rotring pen and a can of cow gum (look it up!) ready to cure the world of crap design. Oh the naivety of youth!

A year later the whole world had decided that, along with Fleet Street and the typesetters there, my job was now going to be done by a computer. Most of what I had learned was going to be completely irrelevant. Luckily I was also taught to use my brain and solve design problems on paper first; rather than hope that a Mac, Photoshop® and F7 would come up with the designs. Nevertheless there was still this question that bugged me and my colleagues…"Why is there so much crap design out there?".

Why would a business use three letters for a company name that meant nothing to their customers and had no connection to anything they are promoting?

Why would a company have a logo that was taken from clipart and was used by three other companies in the same town, let alone the same country?

Why would someone send out flyers or have a brochure that looked completely different in design, so no one could tell if it was the same company?

An answer slowly presented itself once I started to tout my newly acquired skills to prospective customers. It became more defined over the years that I've been developing brand strategies…

"Most people don't care."

Well, that was my initial assessment of the situation and how the interaction with clients seemed to me. I then stepped back for a while and figured these entrepreneurs and go-getters of our future business community can't just "not care". They've taken a huge leap of faith to go self-employed and chase a dream; and they've seen Virgin, M&S and Sainsbury's branding. So what was going on? I then refined my first statement to:

"Most people don't know how much they should care."

This point of view gave me a lot more hope and scope to educate my clients. I had fallen into the same trap as my customers and was acting exactly as they do towards their customers.

Because I know why branding is important to a business, I assumed the businesses I dealt with would know that as well. A lot of businesses I have dealt with over the years know exactly what they do and how they do it. So in turn they assume their customers should just buy from them. "You want a drink, I sell drink.", what more is there to explain?

Well, there's so much more to that transaction than meets the eye and we'll tackle that over the coming pages. So please hang in there!

I had stumbled upon the first cornerstone "Not knowing how much you should care.", which can be forgiven. As with the four stages of learning, this is an example of "unconscious incompetence". You can be forgiven for not knowing about something you don't know about! There were five other behaviours that also contributed to the cornerstones of crap - ones that move into the conscious realm of competence or incompetence. And that's less forgivable!

2 - Cost vs value

The second cornerstone was the bane of most start-up businesses, and indeed a pain to most of us in life, "Money" or rather the lack of it!

Why pay someone to design you a logo when you can get a free image or icon in your latest version of PowerPoint®? Why pay an experienced professional to create a name for your new business when your three initials or your daughter's middle name will do fine! It seems most vans driving round town just have three initials, so that must be the thing to do, right? Yes, you've guessed I'm being a little facetious, but after a couple of decades these criteria crop up the most.

Short-term thinking is a reasonable business survival technique, especially for a start-up in the early days. After all, 50% of you reading this book who are about to start your new venture (according to FORBES) won't make it further than a year, 80% after five years. Understandably, choosing to spend what money you have on a van and some essential tools over a logo and a website may certainly seem the right decision at the time.

3 - Blurred lines of technology

The third fly in the ointment seems to crop up in most creative fields, and far more so since technology gave everyone the ability to be an "expert". If you have a computer, tablet or a smart phone (therefore everyone!) you can now call yourself a "photographer", an "illustrator", a "video editor", a "music composer" or "graphic designer" for that matter. Thanks to Messrs. Gates and Jobs, people think they are just as much an expert as the professionals they engage, "cos we all use the same software". The concept that we have different brains and many years additional knowledge and experience becomes somewhat moot! This modern dilemma of access for everyone is great on one hand and consequently not so good on the other. The line between professional and amateur, especially in the professions I just listed, has become very blurred. Don't get me wrong, technology is of course hugely important to the growth of the world. Hell I can't earn a penny without a Mac, smart phone or email anymore. Not quite as bad as straight forward "crap design", but still as annoying and might get worse as time and technology marches on.

4 - Committee compromise

You know it could be better, but the "customer knows best"! The nights I've cried when the seven finance directors fed back their suggestions of how our design could be better! There's a reason we have the expression:

"A camel is a horse designed by a committee."

I don't really think I need to elaborate any more than that. Art and therefore creativity and design isn't created by a committee. Art has a singular vision. Yes, there may be a team in operation in some circumstances, but with a visionary at the helm.

Take the two massive opportunities we've had in the past 20 years to showcase this country's creativity. The Millennium Dome (clearly in 2000) and the 2012 Olympics. The dome was an embarrassment and a complete failure with government and business committees involved at every level; with several people, supposedly in charge, getting sacked and replaced. The 2012 Olympic opening ceremony led by one creative genius, Danny Boyle. The envy of the entire planet. I rest my case.

5 - They always choose the crap option

To my shock, the fifth part of the puzzle is nothing to do with the owner of the new business and it's actually down to the likes of me and the design industry I represent, when we first start out. I've worked with numerous other graphic designers and branding specialists over the years. We swapped many stories, like most businesses, and one kept repeating itself…

"Why do clients always pick the crap option?"

I remember saying this to my business partner often, or when I would mentor a new designer they would say after presenting several logos to a client:

"As always, they went with the crap one!"

There were two things going on here. One I still have no answer for. Out of say four choices of logos why would a client choose the worst one? I don't know. It could be we have different brains, different criteria of what is "good" or "crap". Different associations, upbringing, the list is endless. The second problem here took quite some time to work out, and then one day it hit me. If the client chose a "crap" logo, then there must have been a "crap" one to choose from. So why did the designer knowingly offer a "crap" logo in the first place?

So to put on my sleuthing deerstalker again, I had to look back and see how I operated in my early days, and see if my actions mirrored other designers. They did! When a designer starts out it seems we are all very eager to please and to show how much work we do for the tiny amount of money we are charging. In being eager to please we show all the options, even the not so good ones. So that's HOW "crap" ones were able to be chosen. WHY they were always chosen is still a mystery! To a seasoned gambler, the odds would seem incredibly high!

This book is really aimed at the new business owners who want to understand why a strong branding strategy is essential for their success.

However, if you are a graphic designer who also wants to pick up some tips, then please take this on board: ONLY present your absolute best designs, three maximum! Do not show everything you've done. Have the confidence that your top ones will do the job. To the business owners who are going to engage a designer I'll give the same advice, only ask for three logos to be presented to you. That should focus the designer to do their very best rather than offer some sketch that they weren't really "feeling" but thought they should show it, "cos it looks like they've done lots of work!".

6 - Blue sky blinkering

The final nail in the coffin is the constant battle between designer and client. To be blunt it's that universal raging war between an abundance of imagination versus an abyss from the lack of it. Well that was always my immediate thought, but the years have mellowed me and some of the fight has evaporated. I now believe it's mainly "fear of creativity" that drives home the last cornerstone. This is a cautionary tale that designers may find hard to swallow, but a useful insight nonetheless.

For a client, engaging the services of someone creative can become a journey into a strange paradox. The very reason to hire a creative brain is because of their divergent or associative thinking capacity or ability. Divergent, meaning a certain type of brain that can come up with more than one answer to the same question, sadly a process that is often educated out of most children (please search for Sir Ken Robinson TED talks). This ability, especially when it comes to creating a logo for instance, is absolutely crucial.

Say your client was a heating engineer or an estate agent, for the sake of getting trademark for instance. They really need you to come up with a logo that's not "a combination of a water drop and a flame" or "a house". The paradox is that to them, the aforementioned hot flame and cold droplet or depiction of a house in some way shape or form is the ONLY answer; and whatever else you come up with isn't the answer they have in their head. So in the client's mind, you're going to have the "wrong" answer.

Clients and businesses say they want "blue sky thinking" or want you to "think outside the box". For a creative, that's an obvious starting point. But to someone who can't think divergently or associatively, that statement is a massive leap into the unknown. Unfortunately, their idea of "thinking outside the box" is a million miles away from a creative one's. And that's because creativity is relative.

It's like asking a philatelist and an adrenalin junkie to suggest doing something daring. You will get two wildly different ideas, from placing stamps in a non-chronological order in an album to base jumping off a live volcano. The fear factor that enters into this exchange of creativity is that if the client doesn't "get it" then they suppose that their customers won't "get it".

Here's the bitter pill: they are probably right. Extreme divergent thinking (at "genius" level) is only shared amongst about 2% of the population. So as a designer, you are going to have to accept that your creativity is not going to be appreciated or understood by the majority of the people you work for.

There is light at the end of the tunnel. Your experience and examples of other people's creativity will eventually build up enough evidence to suggest that being different or original will always help a business more than being the same. If you can argue that, it doesn't matter if the audience doesn't "get it" (whatever the "it" is). They don't need to. They just need to differentiate "it" from the competition and recall "it" easily. This is why we discuss difference and originality in other chapters.

Summon the soothsayer!

That's the first half of the story where we've pinpointed why, through no real fault of their own, start-ups can have bad or non-existent branding strategies; and therefore have the potential to present "crap" marketing material to try and promote themselves. As a designer, how was I going to be able to turn that tide? When will the unconscious incompetence become conscious? When will the money be available? When will the blurred lines start to come into focus?

Well, in my case the answer to that is when the businesses are three to five years into their trading lives. Again, something became apparent in our branding company when we turned to a referral marketing strategy to attract more business. We were being recommended to help businesses around the three to five year period time and time again, but for three quite distinctive reasons.

The big one, with hindsight (the most annoying of sights!) is they realised they should have done it "properly" from the start. Something that you can only learn over time. And because, as we mentioned, other more pressing decisions had to be made without the help of a fortune teller.

The second complaint that came to us was the realisation that the markets these businesses traded in had either become crowded or they noticed their competition had "better branding". Combined with that, their customers were being described as indifferent, not loyal, or wanting cheaper products or services. All these points will be discussed throughout the book.

The last point was a more positive note, as we were being referred to help businesses who were doing "O.K." but wanted to grow, get a second outlet or franchise. Having learned a bit about branding they came to us to see if theirs could be stronger in order to support their visions for growth.

We eventually concluded that if 80% of our clients started to come to us after three to five years in business, there wasn't much we could do about the "crap design" that was being proliferated from day one of a start-up's life. It was always going to happen if we had to trade our expertise, knowledge and experience for a few thousand pounds.

And then it hit me!

Turn the equation around! Offer that wealth of experience and knowledge to thousands of people for a very small amount of money and businesses will have a much better, far more affordable idea on how to implement a branding strategy. You'll know why you should care, you only need to forego the price of two pints of beer for a five-year branding strategy packed with 25 years of expertise, anecdotes, examples and experience. You can actually call yourself an expert without any compromise. Crucially, you'll be three to five years ahead of your competitors (as long as they don't read this book!).

Surely this is a much better way to eradicate "crap" design?

Let's see!

THAT'S MINE, GET OFF!
A BRIEF HISTORY OF BRANDING

You've probably heard of "branding" cattle with a hot poker. And you would be right in thinking that the action of marking someone's property with this method is definitely in the roots of why we associate the practice with the modern form of graphically branding household products.

It is a very literal term from an old Norse word "brandr" meaning "to burn". Anything that could have an owner's symbol or motif burned on it goes way back to 2000 BC (or whatever the version of that is these days). It would include timber, crockery, animals, even slaves and was a way of saying *"This belongs to me, so hands off!"*. It was by no means a way of protecting copyright or trademark, however. That took another 3,876 years (roughly!).

In 1876, the first ever UK registered trademark was (the now very recognisable) red triangle of The William Bass Brewery company. That's not to say that this was the first instance of using a logo to distinguish a product. It was simply that they were first in the queue since the UK Trademarks Act was passed as law.

Bass had been using their red, blue and white triangles since the 1850s, and not surprisingly many other companies the world over have been using text and imagery to do their best to distinguish themselves from their competition. What is interesting is the shift of perception from:

"It's mine, don't touch.".

To:

"Mine's better than theirs, so buy mine!"

With the added and implied caveat of:

"And if you try to copy my symbol, I'm suing.".

If you look back at early examples of product marketing and packaging you'll find they were quite text heavy. This may have been fine for a target market who could actually read. If your audience couldn't read then something like a bright red triangle was a much better way of standing out from the crowded beer labels and attracting your customers, perhaps?

It may not surprise you that the rise of branding, marketing and especially packaging as we know it today really started taking off with the invention of the printing press from 1440. This was a process that enabled printing on flat surfaces. So printing on bottles or biscuit tins had to wait a lot longer when rotary presses came along in the 19th century. The industry had to then wait until the early 20th century to be able to produce good quality photographs once halftone technology came along.

So it turns out that what we recognise as modern branding has actually come a long way in quite a short time. The two other great accelerators to "global" branding were: Firstly the growing opportunities to travel further, quicker and cheaper through trains, ships and planes. And secondly, the insatiable appetite for technology that now enables us to communicate with practically anyone you like anywhere in the world at any time. I think Martini used something similar as a slogan back in the day!

My personal feeling is that those fantastic strides of "efficiency" to make the whole world instantly obtainable from the comfort of your own smart phone haven't necessarily made our lives any more efficient. We've just used all the time we could have relaxed in to create and deliver more "stuff" because the technology has allowed it. So we've saved nothing. I feel that's a philosophical discussion for another time.

Whether there's a causal link or not, at the point in time of putting this book together, logo design has become simpler and simpler. You may already be aware of how logos have evolved over time from intricate wood engraved illustrations to more graphic representations of the former designs.

The urge to simplify or iconise an image or concept to represent a business, product or idea can easily be seen in logo creation these days.

Our modern techno-led platforms should now be a major consideration when beginning to think about designing a logo and brand elements. As well as adorning the side of a building, your logo also has to be quite clear as a Facebook or LinkedIn profile image, and even at 32 pixels square at the top of your internet browser, known as a 'favicon'.

You can't simply do what you want. There is a very much stronger element of conforming if your brand is to work well for you. Understanding these conformities isn't necessarily limiting design choices. The limits of technology have always been with us. It's what drives us to be more creative and invent technology that pushes us forward. We had colour photos and colour TV but couldn't have colour newspapers because of the limitations of technology - until it was fixed. The boundaries in which we design give us the scope to do what we can; and that's useful to explore how to be different within those given rules.

Through this book we will explore what I feel are essential "blocks" you will need to build a strong brand in today's terms. The point being that the meaning behind the word "brand" has clearly morphed over the centuries and more specifically over the last century or so.

Where are we now?

Yes, it was a hot branding iron or tool that enabled you to brand your cattle, and therefore place a recognisable mark on your possessions. In this context, brand could therefore only relate to a symbol, motif or logo (that word logo has a whole other history which we won't go into at the moment).

These days, however, brand sometimes doesn't mean just your logo. It has many other associations and interpretations.

Is it something you see?

Substituting the word brand with the word logo often happens, whomever you may talk to. Within the business environment they will say *"What do you think of my brand?"* pointing at their logo on their business card. It might be just the logo they are pointing out. But the typeface, the colours, perhaps an accompanying image or graphic, may be adding to the look and feel of what they are describing as their brand. So, maybe it's not just a logo.

Is it something you buy?

People who aren't particularly in a business environment often use the word brand when describing generic household products like detergent, cosmetics, cereals etc. You can go to Sainsbury's and they will offer to "brand match" any product you buy elsewhere.

In this context they are differentiating between products produced by well-known manufacturers like Heinz or Kellogg's and their own supermarket produced products which are usually cheaper. The commonly accepted convention here is Heinz is an "original brand" and Sainsbury's produce their "own brand" products. Hang on a minute though! Sainsbury's is also known as a brand in itself. So we may have another category that covers a service or more simply: a business can therefore be described as a brand.

Is it something you sense?

I remember slowly being awoken by strong product branding when I used to catch Formula One racing on TV. I would watch James Hunt in his Marlboro McLaren (showing my age here) but having no realisation that the Marlboro bit was a brand/product produced by the Phillip Morris cigarette company sponsoring the team.

That was, of course, way before cigarette advertising was banned. I then recognised that the likes of Henry Cooper, Kevin Keegan and Leonard Rossiter (who??) would attract their own type of sponsorship and the product companies would want these celebrities to endorse their products. I must stress that this celebrity endorsement was nothing new in my teens back in the late 1970s. I'm merely relating my realisation to you. So someone well known who agreed to endorse a product, was in effect that product's mark - the mere association of that celeb made you think of the product or service or business. As described above, just like a logo being an indelible mark in your mind, such endorsement became a sort of brand.

Is it ubiquitous?

Yes, the concept of brand is absolutely everywhere. It has so many definitions it's now very hard to define as a singular idea. It will mean something different to you than it does to someone else.

As described in the last paragraph, well-known celebrities reminded you of a certain brand. A little time later, we are aware that celebrities themselves are their own brand. Artists, pop stars, athletes, global business owners are now big brands or the "No.1" brand in their field.

From Martha Stewart to David Beckham; or Kanye West to Gwyneth Paltrow, they are known as brands. This is often because they can now endorse their own products, not just be associated with other companies' merchandise as they did back in my day. Perfumes, cooking sauces, clothing, eye ware… you name it, you can buy a product with a celeb's name or mark on it.

What is it not?

Perhaps a slightly facetious question, but just take a look around and describe the everyday objects you see without associating them with the idea of a brand… It's quite hard not to. I've got an IKEA Billy, holding my Waterstones book, leaning against my Homebase wallpaper, coated with Dulux paint, that also has a DFS sofa next to it, with my cat sleeping on it. HA!! My cat is not a brand, except that it's wearing a collar marking it as belonging to me. So we come full circle!

I think that sequence of paragraphs enlightens us to why trying to understand what branding is becomes a minefield. It is many things to different people. I do a lot of networking and when I wear a badge that says what I do, it says "logos and stuff" and not "branding". When I had the word branding on my badge, so many people were baffled. They didn't really know what I could do for them or how my services, as someone who does branding, could benefit them.

This is not surprising, if for instance, they thought I could give them a better price on detergent from Sainsbury's; or I could help an athlete become No.1 in their field. People, in the main, get what a graphic designer does and how that profession helps businesses. I studied to be one, got a degree in the subject and was employed by two companies as one before I set up my business.

I certainly started out as a graphic designer, but found I had to offer more value to my clients if my business was to progress. And that offering of "value" is also one of the key components of a brand. So my leap from graphic designer to branding consultant allowed me to get far more involved with the goals and aspirations of a business by creating their branding strategies as well as their logo.

Anyway, grasping the value behind a great branding strategy is what this book will be exploring, so let's move on.

SO YOU THINK YOU'VE GOT AN IDEA?

SOME THINGS TO CONSIDER BEFORE YOU LEAVE YOUR JOB

As a "nation of shopkeepers" this isle should be very proud of the independent business owners who quite literally keep this country going. In 2020 SMEs (small to medium sized enterprises) and a newly termed "micro business", made up 99.9% of the businesses in the UK. They also contributed to 61% of employment in the private sector and contributed to 52% of the UK's annual turnover equating to £2.3 trillion! I don't know about you, but I'm impressed by those stats! An SME is anything from a one man band (OMB) or politely termed "owner managed business" all the way up to 250 employees or around £40 million turnover. Which to most of us is actually quite BIG! We all have to start somewhere and that's something I constantly have to remind my clients. All the so called big companies with huge globally successful brands were OMBs once just like them, let's not forget that.

It's also incredibly tricky in the early months and years for all kinds of reasons that a well-designed logo won't ever help you with. One big area that can seem a barrier to growth is the very thing that will enable your growth, and that's employees. Employment law is an absolute minefield and gets more and more complicated each and every year as our society becomes more "enlightened". Sometimes it feels incredibly weighted against the employer and I'm sure there's a few nodding heads here. But that is the reality of running a modern business, and protecting your employees is no bad thing. In fact looking after your staff is pivotal to building your brand. Mr Brand himself, Richard Branson, is credited with the quote:

"Look after your staff and they'll look after your customers."

He only said that in 2015, but I'm sure this kind of concept has been uttered previously. I say that because it's something I've said for years.

I have preferred working with B2C (business to consumer) businesses which is all about serving the customer face-to-face, as opposed to an online business or a faceless corporate. A coffee shop, a hairdresser, a garage, for instance. If your staff are having a bad day or aren't happy at work they could reflect that onto your customers. In turn, your customers' experience won't be as good as it could have been. Those customers then tell their friends of their recent experience through the ultra-effective marketing technique called "word of mouth". You may have heard of word of mouth marketing or referral marketing. It is very effective as it relies on trust, where most other marketing techniques can't do that at the start. The problem with bad word of mouth marketing (or gossip as it's also known) is that it travels 11 times quicker than good word of mouth! This fact alone should be enough for a business owner to treat their staff incredibly well. Unfortunately, as you and I know and have experienced, customer service in the UK is, at best, a mixed bag! I urge you to hold on to Richard Branson's quote.

You may have picked up this book a few years down the line in your business, or you may be thinking about starting a new venture. Either way I hope it gives you plenty to think about and I will be asking you lots of questions with space for you to put down your answers! A business dream will have far more chance succeeding when you start writing things down. If the answers stay in your head, then so will the dream.

For this chapter, on the one hand I'll assume you are a start-up and "*you think you have a good business idea*". Hopefully you haven't gone too far down the line and are happy to read on!

On the other hand, if you are a few years into your business, I'll also assume "*you THOUGHT you had a good business idea*" but it hasn't quite gone to plan and perhaps something in this book might help. I truly hope so.

Do your research

I won't beat around the bush. Lack of research is a major reason why business ideas fail (the actual business may not, but the stats coming reflect actual businesses). Have you seen *Dragon's Den*? I've lost count of the times Peter Jones or Deborah Meaden has said: "*You've solved a problem that doesn't exist - I'm out.*". They say a lot of other things, but that suits this part of the chapter!

Forbes, the American business magazine also cites 42% of start-ups fail because of the "*lack of market need for their product*". UK stats don't fair that well either: 20% of businesses fail in the first year, up to 50% by year two and nearly 90% by the fifth year. Of course, there will be 101 reasons why businesses or their ideas fail. The trackable stats between those failures and the lack of research into a marketplace should be sobering enough to realise that it's not going to be easy. As I plead with you to think about research, you may be pleading with me, asking: "*What kind of research needs to be done?*".

Let us first ascertain where you are with your idea. Later on I'll discuss "reputation" which explores a business model built on just that: your reputation. Your idea could be quite simple, you have some innate quality, skill, acumen for something and people (by that I mean friends) have asked for your help or advice. They have been extremely grateful and have possibly told a friend about you and their experience of you. You might realise at this point that you are of value to other people, you have something they don't have and it's something they need. And, by the way, this is a strong basis for a brand. Lack of something, or scarcity creates demand, supply of that demand is one fundamental of any business transaction and that really helps with valuing that supply. The more scarce or, the more "lack of supply", the higher the price.

At some point in time you have created a reputation for being *"handy with a can of paint"* or *"knowing the ins and outs of double book entering"* or *"clever when it comes to tinkering under a car bonnet"*. In this scenario, your good business idea is: *"I could do this for a living and leave my day job"*.

The reason you might be having such a thought is that your friends and their contacts have given you a few quid or a bottle of red to thank you for helping them out. They have valued your special gift for changing a spark plug. It's no great leap to surmise that if you charged a bit more than a few quid and dispensed your skill more frequently you may have a business on your hands, and you'd be perfectly within your rights to think that. So before summoning up the strength to tell your existing boss what you really think of them and where they can shove the nine to five, set aside some time to do some detective work about your next move.

Are they just being nice?

The blunt answer is YES. With any business decision, the worst thing you can do is ask your friends or family for advice or even just an opinion. The exception is your spouse, if you have one at this "moment of clarity", who is more likely to be honest or at least be affected. Your friends and family are the least objective and most under qualified people to go to; but in my experience, for sub-conscious psychological reasons, always the first port of call. When I've presented a new company name or a new logo to a business, I explicitly ask my clients to not ask their friends and family for feedback, and here's why.

First of all it's not fair on them. How on earth can they give an informed and qualified opinion on a new name for instance when they haven't gone through the briefing meeting, haven't done the research and have zero experience on naming companies? Secondly, it's not fair on you to make a decision based on advice built on a crossed finger and a belief that a shared set of genes somehow trumps every other source of knowledge.

So, to make myself clear, asking friends and family if your decision to "go it alone" is not enough research. This common route is more about reaching out to find a reassuring "yes" to a decision that you have probably already convinced yourself to go with. You will lock on to all the "yeses" you hear, and mystically ignore the "no's". Even if your friends and family don't think it's a good idea, the impossible position you may have put them in might make them say something like:

"If it's what you really want, then you should.", or:

"I probably wouldn't but I'm not you, so go for it.".

You heard two "yeses" when in fact there were two "no's". One caveat to the above is, if a family member or friend has started their own business then the rationale for asking advice may be more about querying the pitfalls of running any business, rather than your specific business idea. Your friend may be in a completely different market and therefore would face very different hurdles, but will share some thoughts on the basics.

Another reason to seek help is if you are going into the same market as your friend. This is potentially awkward as you are suggesting to go into direct competition with them. Depending on their outlook on life they could get defensive and therefore tell you it's an awful idea, so that's not helpful or even truthful. I believe there can always be collaboration with any perceived competition, so tread carefully and see where there might be some win-win options.

If the friends and family research is off limits, as I am suggesting, then we should turn to the proper term. Businesses like to call it market research. I want to break down jargon in the fields of marketing and branding in this book and explain them in the most basic way I can. So we'll start here with some typical marketing jargon alongside my suggested explanation.

Given your inherent skill or ability:

1. **Are you entering an original, niche or crowded market?** Does anybody, apart from your friends, need your skill and can you provide evidence to support this assumption?
2. **What's the market sector size and who is your target audience?** How many people do you think need your skill and can you describe who they are by age or gender or any other type of category?
3. **Who are your competitors?** Who else, near you, already offers your skill?
4. **What's the price point?** How much do these other people charge for their (and therefore your) skill?
5. **What are the geographic boundaries to your product or service?** How far are you willing to travel or your customers willing to travel for your skill, or is it available online?
6. **Can you diversify or expand your product or**

service? What other businesses out there offer your skill as part of a bigger range of skills?

7. **Where will you position yourself in your market?** Are people sort of offering your skill but not quite as good or as fast or as well priced? Or are some much better, quicker or cheaper than you?
8. **What are your differentiating messages?** Can you find reviews of how good, bad or indifferent other people are with a similar skill as yours?
9. **What's your marketing strategy?** How are other people getting their customers?
10. **What's your branding strategy?** How are other people with your skill presenting themselves?

If you spent just a day answering those questions you would already be representing a business that has done more market research than a good 90% of start-ups. So you have given yourself a massive chance of succeeding longer than you did before you picked up this book. A cursory glance online for instance will certainly scratch the surface of most of those questions. If you fancy being a decorator, just type "decorator" and your home town and bang, you have an answer to number one in terms of the supply of your skill locally as well as an answer to number three, as you can now see your perceived competition and so on. Some business sectors, like decorating or other trades, tend not to have their own websites but there are plenty of directory websites like FreeIndex or Checkatrade for instance that help with your competitive analysis research. I'm getting all jargony again!

I'm flabbergasted when a client has come to us for some branding advice and have already "come up" with a name. I ask, *"Did you Google it?"* (brand name alert, there are other search engines available) to see if someone else may have come up with it before. So please do that!

An entire book can be devoted to each of those ten (and a lot more) research questions. So I'm not suggesting that we've summed up all there is to know when considering market research, not by any stretch of the imagination.

However, this book is going to devote itself to question number ten:

'What's your branding strategy?'

The answers to this particular question, when I've posed it via customer focus groups, are extraordinarily varied. They have made me really consider that a lot of people starting a business do not understand branding at all, something I've already touched on in the first chapter of this book.

Most business ideas are not new. In fact very little in business or life is completely original. Different variations, slight improvements, yes, but completely original is hard to come by. Trying to get people to buy into original is often a hard slog, especially if it completely destroys all competition. Or it loses the government, or their big business funders, money. I'm getting all conspiracy theorist now I'll stop! But do look up "suppressed inventions".

Where was I? ...ah yes! An original way of approaching something old is a different matter though, and that's what this book will attempt to help you with.

There was beer before Bass. There were vacuum cleaners before Dyson. There was furniture before IKEA and these comparisons can go on and on.

If you have come up with something completely original that has never been done before, like perpetual motion or time travel, then you're going to need a lot more help than this book can offer. However, if you have a skill or business idea that has been done before, you are going to need to convince your prospective customers that your particular way of providing this product or service is somehow different. The difference can be tiny or huge, simple or complicated, implied or perceived. But it will need to be clear and relevant to your potential customer.

The next ten chapters will hopefully give you the rationale that will help you describe, package and showcase that difference in the best light possible. You'll have the ability to create a credible brand that will attract the right audience and set you apart from your competition. Your customers will buy INTO your skill, product or service and believe your original approach to something familiar is a better, reliable and a more valuable choice.

Sharp intake of breath.

THE TEN BUILDING BLOCKS

Passion
Promise
Reputation
Name
Original
Different
Appropriate
Perception
Consistent
Value

#1 PASSION

NEVER WORK A DAY IN YOUR LIFE

#1 - A BRAND IS PASSION

I've tried to place my Top Ten "A brand is…" answers in order of importance to me, but they could be mixed up depending on where you are on your business journey. The order is also a prompt list I tend to go through when facing a new client and defining a brief. So this should flow for you as if we're meeting for the first time and chatting about your new venture!

A few of the reasons for writing this book were prompted by the odd frank exchange of views I've had with prospective clients. Don't get me wrong, I'm not using this book to vent any frustrations - cos we all have our opinions, and different approaches work for different people. One such minor difference of opinion was the sentiment behind this chapter's title. The extended turn of phrase would be, "If you love what you do, you'll never have to work a day in your life". This particular client couldn't have disagreed more and suggested he had been told that to succeed in business you have to be completely objective and disconnected about your product or service. He went on to suggest that being passionate about it would only distract you, make you lose focus and cloud any business decisions or judgements that have to be made.

"*Hmmm…*" I thought, "*this could be interesting.*".

I had two choices: back down, agree and just sign him up. Or listen further, put my thoughts across, win him over and then sign him up!

Well, because I'm passionate about my profession, I of course described why being passionate about what you do is an absolute fundamental foundation for developing a brand. Listening further to the business owner in front of me, I slowly began to understand where he was coming from. And it drilled down to one simple factor or difference. We were both describing two different models or approaches to business, neither of us were right or wrong.

He was describing how to "grow a business".

I was talking about "building a brand".

He wanted customers to buy FROM him.

I wanted his customers to buy INTO him.

Growing a business is fundamentally easy (I say that knowing it's not!). Ultimately your outgoings need to be less than your incomings. If you've read any books about business, it's not about turnover or profit, it's all about cashflow. However, if all your focus is about getting people to just buy FROM you, then you and your competitors will get locked into lowering prices until one of you goes out of business.

Brands don't do that!

A well-known brand is never the cheapest. It has to offer more than price.

In fact, a strong brand takes price off the table. It knows not to be stupid, it might push it a bit too far sometimes, but for other reasons, we forgive them and keep coming back.

I carried on with the conversation…

There are plenty of successful dispassionate businesses out there that none of us have heard of. That, I don't deny. My proposition is that the thousands of businesses that we have heard of, are almost always brands that we (or should I say the target audience) love. Their customers have an affinity with the product or service. They often share the same values, philosophies and passions as the owners.

Naturally I'm going to cite Apple for being passionate about "thinking differently". But also The Body Shop for being passionate about not testing on animals, Volvo for their passion for safety, Innocent for their passion of additive-free drinks and CO-OP for their passion for fair trade and so on. I'm sure you have your own favourite brands you prefer, some more than others of course. We all have to buy necessities like soap and loo roll for instance, and may not think we're drawn to certain products because of a shared passion. This would be true in many cases. If the supermarket or corner shop is closer, then distance and convenience becomes the driver. You may even be influenced by what you've been brought up on by your parents and not even realise it.

You don't have to live or die for the products you buy, but having a preference to buy FROM one company or a product as opposed to another is often down to more than the price. It starts to enter into the realms of buying INTO something else. Making the most of that reason helps you attract more of the right type of customer and that helps build the brand awareness of your company, service or product, by those customers spreading the good word. Amen!

So I'm asking you to consider the concept of placing your passion at the heart of your new venture. Firstly to make sure you can remind yourself you're doing what you're doing because you love it so much. And secondly because you can use your passion to tell a story. Such a story will inform everything you do - especially when it comes to marketing your business. More of that later.

The Inquisition

I have three test questions I ask business owners to essentially frame their passion and give it some purpose. So see if you can answer these questions:

1. Why do you get up every morning?
2. How are you going to change the world?
3. What do you stand for?

If you answered quickly and without thinking too hard then congratulations, you're in the elite 1% (ish) who can manage that! If you found the questions hard or even ridiculous, then you're in good company!

QUESTION ONE
WHY DO YOU GET UP EVERY MORNING?

There are plenty of reactions to this question, amongst them are:

1. To go to work

2. Pay off the mortgage/bills

3. Back ache

4. The alarm clock wakes me up

5. To walk the dog…

Close?

If you haven't heard of Simon Sinek, please look him up. He is a great marketing consultant and motivational speaker. If you have heard of him you may know about his talks and views about "The WHY" when it comes to business. I've been banging on about the WHY for about ten years before he "owned it" but them's the breaks!

Anyway, Mr Sinek points out that the vast majority of businesses concentrate on WHAT they do or produce. He suggests that companies with great leadership concentrate on the WHY.

My approach certainly dovetails with that, except I have always emphasised that great brands were all about the WHY. The truth is, it's both. But what are we both actually on about?

Well, we're on about the "Passion" of course. WHY should you get up in the morning? Because you love what you do and you can't wait to do what you love doing every morning. If you get up because you have to pay the mortgage and that therefore becomes your rationale and your own mindset for your business, then I ask: "*What customer in their right mind, is going to buy into that?*".

Your customers know WHAT you do. Even your prospective customers know what you do, that's why they've Googled you or walked into your shop or showroom or other establishment. You don't need to tell them you sell cars or coffee, they're not stupid. I know it sounds odd and I'm slightly exaggerating for effect. But what I'm pointing out is that too many businesses spend a disproportionate amount of time or budget on WHAT they sell when they should consider more ways to shout about WHY they sell their product or service.

In essence: Market the passion, share the story.

QUESTION TWO
HOW ARE YOU GOING TO CHANGE THE WORLD?

This question should lead on nicely from question one. So as to not scare you too much, I'm not asking you to commit to eliminating poverty or create world peace. Again, it's a question to make you agitate your neurons a little. We can all help change the world for the good, or for the bad, and as the adage goes, "You can eat a whole elephant one bite at a time.". To put the question into a more manageable size, smiling at a stranger is changing the world... one smile at a time!

I mentioned Anita Roddick's company, The Body Shop, where most of us are aware that she was passionate about tackling cruelty to animals and determined to do her bit to cut down on that practice... one rabbit at a time!

Taking that scenario, answering question one easily leads to answering question two.

The normal default for the HOW in business, asks how are you going to sell me this car or coffee? A company might promote fuel savings or extra marshmallows, for instance. This type of HOW equates to the USPs or differences from a competitor. Again, I'm not saying ignore these factors - they are of course important. As with question one, I'm merely pointing out that there are more messages to focus on than the standard defaults. The more emotional, philosophical, passionate messages you can share with your audience, the more you can connect with them, especially if your competition are just saying: *"Hey, we sell cars, want one that goes a little bit faster?"*.

QUESTION THREE
WHAT DO YOU STAND FOR?

This question is a little more obvious, but still quite telling at the same time. It's there to ask you about your ethical or moral VALUES. Hopefully you'll have some! These are distinct from the monetary value of a business. We'll be discussing both in the last building block. Like passion, VALUES are a bit more fluffy, but please stick with me! This question is there to identify more personal attitudes to how you already conduct yourself within this world, and how your own values can steer the practices and decisions in your business.

Before you start to write them down, please be aware of some values that are basic prerequisites for business, like: honesty, transparency, customer service, professionalism, "truth and justice for all". When I see those "company values" on a meeting room wall, I die just a little bit more!

I can't tell you what your values are or WHAT you stand for. But at some point in the growth of your business or rather, the building of your brand, you will be doing things like:

- Making decisions
- Marketing to your customers
- Sub-contracting
- Recruiting
- Managing and giving responsibility to your staff

Your value system, if well-defined and deeply rooted, will help you with these things enormously. Let's suggest you have values like:

- Responsibility
- Communication
- Rewarding
- Empowering
- Ethical
- Peaceful
- Supportive
- Determined
- Playful
- Methodical, etc.

By sharing your values, be that verbally, by your actions or just pinned on a cork board for all to see, you'll create a culture built around those values. Deciding who to recruit, who to work with or how to deal with customers becomes easier when guided by your values. Employees, in particular, are able to buy into a company philosophy when the cultural values are clearly showcased. In turn they then demonstrate those values to the customer. This shows a consistency throughout the whole business, which is very important to a customer. Anyway, a lot more about consistency and values in further chapters.

I think that's Passion done. It's a biggie for me so I hope it wasn't too indulgent! I just hope you do love what you do and if it's a case of "not minding" what you do, then I really hope this helps you to rediscover what you once loved with a renewed confidence.

PASSION - STRATEGY QUESTIONS

1. Why do you get up every morning? Simply describe what you're passionate about and you can start to market your story.

2. How are you going to change the world? Consider how your business can positively impact the world, one customer at a time - and you can start differentiating yourself and hone your messaging.

3. What do you stand for? Write your values down and share them. Stay true to them and all decision making becomes easier.

#2 PROMISE

THE PROMISED LAND

#2 - A BRAND IS A PROMISE

Whether you are just about to start your venture or you're a few years in, I'm hoping this element doesn't come as a surprise. A brand, as we've established in the opening chapters, is described by many people as many different things. Yourself, a box of washing powder, a name, a celebrity, a logo. Yes, it encompasses all those elements. But ultimately, if I had to pin it down to one description and I was forced to not go any further in this book, it would definitely be something like:

"The promise to your customer"

I could stop there, as it's as close as most people in branding have managed to get if you want a quick answer. Having a promise covers "how you build a brand", and "how you keep a brand". However, the answer doesn't quite explain how you might find that promise in the first place or find a promise that is different enough from competitors.

Towards the end of the book is a chapter on Straplines which, in my experience working with SMEs, is a part of branding that is largely ignored. For me, it is more important than the name and the logo. I mention the strapline section because it does work hand in hand with the promise and can often be the one phrase that immediately tells the customer what their promise is. However, a strapline doesn't always have to define a promise. It may just be an instruction to your audience like NIKE'S "Just Do It". Not so much of a promise, more of a way of attracting the right type of determined, serious customer that Nike wish to deal with. Anyway more of that in the strapline chapter!

We also touch on creating a promise appropriate to your brand, and where it's positioned in a crowded market. Sometimes the promise is highly nuanced, sometimes it's mind-blowing. I will discuss other elements that are going to help you build and market your brand as well as maintain or differentiate your brand. Put simply, to maintain your brand you need your customers to keep coming back. So one of many golden rules would be to just keep your promise.

"How do you come up with a promise?" you may be asking. Well, that can be tricky, especially if you're just starting out. You might not even know you have a promise to offer yet. You might have to wait patiently while it slowly presents itself over time, brought about by the transactions and feedback from your customers.

If a strapline could be the customer facing version of a company's promise, we should also consider that a company may have a whole set of internal promises as well, say towards the staff or suppliers. So here's a few things to consider when finding that key promise or set of promises to build your brand and business around.

1. The "don't have a promise" promise

Didn't expect that, did you? I merely put this first in case anyone's thinking that the best way to not break your promise to your customer is to not have one to break. I can't argue with the logic. But I would suggest it's not the best strategy to sell or market yourself, especially against competitors who will undoubtedly be promising something like being: "The quickest", "The friendliest", "The crumbliest"…

2. The "WHY, HOW, WHAT" promise

In the previous chapter we looked at your passion and asked three questions: *"Why do you get up every morning?"*, *"How are you going to change the world?"* and *"What do you stand for?"*. If we take the Anita Roddick example, her passion was to create a range of products that can be produced by not testing on animals. It therefore doesn't take a great leap to translate an internal passion or philosophy into a "Promise". In The Body Shop example, the promise would be that all their products are not tested on animals. That might sound simplistic, but sometimes these things need pointing out! I urge you to keep reminding yourself of your values as this would be a useful starting point, though it might need a little simplification to make the promise more immediate or transferrable.

3. The "under" promise

The one strapline for me which implies the most low level promise of all is Tesco's "Every little helps". It literally suggests that they will do as little as possible in order to help. It would therefore suggest that the promise will be quite easy to keep. This version of a promise is actually a good model, especially as a start-up. Because the one thing you might be keen to do is promise the earth as you may not want to turn down work so early on in your business. The usual problem with that is you may place yourself in a precarious position of letting customers down when you become overworked. However, under promising and over delivering is always the best strategy. Don't put yourself in a situation where keeping your promise becomes difficult. If you know you can deliver something in 30 minutes, promise to do it in an hour. You've had 30 minutes extra time to not make a mistake and the customer could get it 30 minutes earlier than expected. You both win.

4. The "company name" promise

The reason "Name" is one of the building blocks in this book is because it could be the element that defines the agenda of the promise in the clearest way. Take easyJet or Kwik Fit or Kleenex the implied promise is screaming at you. I would imagine that each of these companies did intend to show the benefit of their company within their name, but did they understand that they also created an everyday double-edged sword? If a customer's experience becomes difficult with "easy"Jet then they are instantly off brand. Because the implied promise is ever present in the name, your business has a consistent reminder to focus on making every interaction as "easy" or "kwik" as possible. You're not going to forget.

And that's the crux of it: you are either ON or OFF brand at the point of keeping or breaking that implied promise.

5. The "measurable" promise

The "company name" promise could fall into this category as well, especially, if like Kwik Fit, you start to suggest how quick your quickness is going to be. Back in the day when we used to have our holiday photos processed by Snappy Snaps we were already presented with an implied promise of speed by the ingenious alliteration of the combined benefit and product moniker.

After that we were then offered some more very specific promises of turnaround to get our snaps back. Next day, same day and even within three hours. You may be in a market, where time or speed or price is critical, or better still moveable and you can offer different versions of the same promise. Businesses often call these service level agreements (SLAs). You might see, gold, silver, bronze levels of service or diamond, ruby and sapphire, for instance. Garages offer different service levels, printers offer different turnaround times and adjust the price accordingly. Even the Post Office offers 1st class post, 2nd class or Special Delivery, some carrying paid-for guarantees. These are all very measurable. If the special package doesn't arrive before 12.00, the promise is broken.

6. The "price" promise

To me, this one is quite dangerous if a business is reliant on being the cheapest, but there are some nuances to consider. Take Poundland or Poundstretcher - we're back to an immediate implied promise even with the name. But I mention them in this category because the name centres on price. However in this instance it's not suggesting it's the cheapest. The 99p Store suggests that!

If you've been in one of these types of store you'll know that some things are not simply £1, or perhaps a multiple of items will be sold for £1. So some grey area regarding the implied promise.

The more dangerous promise would be something like "We will never be beaten on price". With this promise you are opening yourself up for some tough scrutiny from your customers, or they are going to take advantage by pretending they can get your product cheaper. You'll then have to put in clauses about geographical distance and age or version of similar products to make sure like is being compared with like. All of which takes time and effort and you could be losing even more margin. On the other hand, you may get more customers coming through the door on the initial marketing of such a promise. Swings and roundabouts I guess.

Different versions of this sort of promise would be to suggest figures like 20% off your next purchase or buy one get one free, and so on.

It's not all about being the cheapest though, like Stella Artois, you could promise to be reassuringly expensive! Some customers want to be seen to be buying the most expensive, so you could tap into that. One promise I've never quite understood is John Lewis's "Never knowingly undersold". I get that if a customer finds the same product elsewhere, John Lewis will refund you the difference. What I've never really understood is the parallel acceptance of John Lewis carrying the kudos of being slightly more expensive than other similar stores. That aside, the concept of "We'll price match" or "Refund the difference" is a marketable promise. No win, no fee for lawyers would be another price promise. I'm sure you can think of others.

7. The "competitive benefit" promise

This category just about covers everything else that the above promises don't quite fall into. We've covered quickest, easiest, cheapest or dearest, so you just need to think of a superlative adjective that you can compete on. Biggest, smallest, tallest, strongest, funniest, happiest, safest…maybe you can even think of companies that already promise these things. Other superlative adjectives that don't end in "est" would be a promise that starts with "the most…" e.g. amazing, beautiful, intelligent, complex, revolutionary and so on.

8. The "emotional interpretive" promise

First of all, I'm not suggesting you promise to make people cry. This category has a far stronger need for customers to buy into the philosophy or ethos of the brand. A stand out promise or strapline came from the telecoms company Orange (now EE) with its "The future's bright, the future's Orange". I would say that this kind of statement is more about creating an inspirational promise that allows the customer to engage on a different level than the previous promises. Apple's "Think different", and Nike's "Just do it" are almost turning the tables onto the customer. There's an implication that the companies themselves promise to act in these ways, but more importantly these companies want you to act this way as well. This sharing of philosophy attracts the audience that these companies want as customers. They want customers who think and behave like them. The inherent promise to the customer is that they will be part of a family, feel welcomed with like-minded people, part of a special gang. Sky's "Believe in better" or L'Oréal's "Because you're worth it" have similar sentiments. Nothing concrete like price or service, just a shared warm fuzzy feeling.

9. The "no holds barred" promise

This kind of promise is a different type of brashness to the superlative adjective and could be just an adjective or something outrageous. Carlsberg lager used to promise that their product was "Probably the best beer in the world". Cleverly (or advised by their lawyer) they did put the word "Probably" in the promise.

However, recently they've had to change their promise because they had to finally admit it wasn't true. Another high profile company with an outrageous promise was Red Bull's "…Gives you wings". Most sensible consumers readily bought into the alignment of Red Bull's extreme or high risk sports. They could take the mental leap that engaging with the product gave them the sense of being associated with high flying risk taking. That was until one consumer (more likely a competitor) legally took them to task and complained that upon drinking the product no wings appeared and the gentleman in question found that he couldn't fly. You may now notice that Red Bull have now added two more "i's" in the word Wings, giving us Wiiings. Slightly sticking a proverbial two fingers to the court decision to amend their implied promise.

Bigger and bolder promises could take the form of BMW's "The ultimate driving machine". If a customer suggests that they've had a better experience in another driving machine I wonder what the recourse is? Much like any of the above promises, if the customer's experience is that you haven't kept your implied promise you are suddenly, at that point, in the mind of the customer, off-brand. So be careful what you promise.

10. The "we're so sorry we broke our" promise

Clearly I've put this in to give us a top 10, as I only had 9! However there will be a time when a customer is disappointed and I do urge you to have systems and processes in place to cope with a broken promise. In fact, counter intuitively, here is where you can create customers for life even more so than simply doing what you promised you would do. Quickly admitting where you've gone wrong and just as quickly offering to fix the problem and possibly doing a bit more on top is where you can really score loyalty points and create great PR. I recall quite recently in 2018 when K.F.C. ran out of chicken and quickly ran a brilliant 'we're sorry' ad campaign rearranging the usual initials on a bucket to 'FCK'. On a slightly smaller scale, Sainsbury's publicly apologised to three year old Lily Robinson who complained that her tiger bread looked more like a giraffe's markings. Sainsbury's very astutely proceed to change the name of their product to giraffe bread. The PR went viral.

Trying to blame everything or everyone around you on why something didn't work out will not help you in the long run. Sort out the problem, offer discounts or freebies or similar incentives and your customer has a great story to tell their friends. It's a great opportunity for some free marketing. But don't rely on it for a complete marketing strategy, you will go out of business!

PROMISE - STRATEGY QUESTIONS

1. What is your promise to your customer? And that can be found in all your messaging or USPs or even in your name or strapline.

2. How are you able to OVER deliver on your promise? This is particularly for start-ups who tend to promise the earth to get lots of new business. Don't overdo it.

3. What systems do you have in place when you can't always keep your promise? Oddly enough, this can sometimes be your greatest opportunity to win customers for life. Bending over backwards when something doesn't go to plan creates great PR.

#3 REPUTATION

MY MATE'S GOOD AT THAT!

#3 - A BRAND IS REPUTATION

I think this could be the shortest chapter, so just put the kettle on and we'll be over before it's boiled.

Put as simply as I can, your reputation is a barometer of how many times you've either kept or broken your promise. It's something you can manage in a reactive manner as opposed to proactively creating the required perception in the first place. More of that building block later.

If you cast your mind back, in the chapter "So you think you've got an idea" we touched on a scenario where the motivation to start a business was built around the fact that you were known to be "good at something". Friends and family had asked you to help out with the decorating, accounts or car problems and they were extremely appreciative and even offered payment in kind or actual cash. "Word" got out and recommendations were coming your way. You hadn't done any advertising or marketing, no website, so what was going on? Well, in essence your "reputation" was preceding you and was creating business opportunities as well as genuine enquiries. So perhaps "You could do this for a living and leave your day job!".

Remember that bit? Great!

Reputation, or at least the "good words and recommendations" in the previous scenario, helped the person consider a leap into setting up a business. Of course, not all businesses start that way. I know people who haven't got a clue about what they are doing but have huge amounts of enthusiasm, a drive to put things into place and surround themselves with people who DO know what they are doing. So you don't need to have a good reputation, or any reputation for that matter, to start a business.

Building on your reputation

As I explained earlier, one of the reasons I wanted to write this book is to try to demystify some of the jargon surrounding branding. Early on in my interactions with clients, I quickly learned not to actually say the word brand so much and instead use the word reputation. They seemed to suddenly get a lightbulb moment. I could use the nearest definition of branding, "the promise to your customer", but better than that I also said I'm not here to build your brand, I'm here to help build your reputation. The two are completely interchangeable. I might have been taught at polytechnic to use the phrase brand awareness, but it made more sense to my clients to say reputational awareness.

To pretty much understand all other variants of "brand" related words I suggest you simply substitute the word reputation. I think it hits harder.

Damaging your brand becomes damaging your reputation, protecting your brand becomes protecting your reputation and so on.

From the feedback you attract from early customers, you may already feel you have the beginnings of a reputation. Ordinarily, someone like me would be asked to help build your brand, so let's twist that and see how you can build on your reputation. If we look at one of the "promise" categories, like number seven, the "competitive benefit" promise, it highlights that you might be known for a superlative. You may well have intentionally decided this superlative was what your service or product was all about, or it's a description that your customers often used. Let's just suppose it's a good word and people aren't saying a bad word to describe you!

My advice here is to pounce on it, push into it, associate yourself with it and own it. Whatever "est" or "most..." you are, then that's one of your differentiators. Try to use the word in your marketing, your emails, your social media posts. Then try to be the "est" in your actions if this is possible, in addition to the core service or product you deliver. Let's not take me too literally though, obviously the Cadbury's Flake team can't be the flakiest when it comes to customer service!

If you've got a reputation for being the "sharpest tool in the box" wear a sharp suit, add some sharp or witty humour to an email. Don't be a tool!

This "est" will increase its association with you, your reputation and therefore your brand.

Holding on to your reputation

You can certainly create a reputation, build on it, keep it; but of course you can also damage or even lose it - ask Gerald Ratner!

Sometimes circumstances out of your control, can let your customers down. Elements of a supply chain, employees, competitors, market forces, for instance. Through no direct fault of your own, a customer's belief in your promise can be broken. What you do about it is crucial. At this very point in time you are "off brand", there's no getting away from that.

But you have a great opportunity to actually build on your reputation.

Compared to your "promise", your "reputation" is a lot harder to handle. We've said before, that it precedes you. Therefore customers you haven't even met may already know of your reputation and may have an opinion of you and your business, product or service - good or bad. Moreover these prospective customers are likely to have been told about you by their friends. Their friends who they trust, respect and may even love. So imagine the emotional connection they have with their friends, and then they are let down by a company who they have transferred that connection to.

When you break a promise or let someone down, emotionally and psychologically they can sometimes feel as if they have let themselves down. That might sound odd but think about this; People will have an expectation of you, based on your perceived promise, it can just as easily be based on that person's expectations of themselves. If you haven't matched their expectation of you and they have misjudged you, then their judgment (which they now own) was wrong. That can make them feel bad about themselves, because they now feel they were wrong to place a higher expectation on you. You may be familiar with people saying:

"I wouldn't eat there if it was the last chance of food in the world!". That emotional language, however exaggerated, does demonstrate how emotionally attached people can be to a company.

Oops... sorry

Damaging your reputation is obviously never your intention (I'd hope). Of late though, the chances of you or your employees damaging your reputation have dramatically increased. Reputations are now collapsing based on a ten-year-old tweet, let alone a late delivery outside a guaranteed time slot or a HelloFresh box with a missing ciabatta. I don't want to be dragged into a discussion on the evils or utopian ideals of the digital age or social media, but life as a business owner is somewhat more complicated than it ever was.

Is your workforce diverse enough?
Has your email server been hacked?
Are your green credentials green enough?
Did you use the right pronouns?
Has someone "sent to all" by mistake?
Are your staff behaving responsibly outside the workplace?
Are all the current legal HR contracts in place?
Are you sure you're GDPR compliant?
Has office banter turned into harassment?

All of these are concerns for a business in 2021, yet none of them has anything to do with the reason you started your business idea in the first place.

You may not cause an oil spillage or a pandemic outbreak in the first years of trading, so let's not get into the hyperbole of the worst possible scenario. The point here is that any reputational damage by definition impacts on your reputation, and in this case let's actually say brand. You may lose staff, who then gossip (if they haven't already before they leave). You may well lose customers. A loss of reputation may hit the selling price of a business if that's an exit strategy.

Yes, things will go wrong or even horribly wrong. The key here is to have some kind of process in place to react as quickly as you can when the unfortunate happens.

Damage recovery

Now if the fast paced reach of the internet or email or social media can quickly disseminate whatever you may have messed up, the same funnel of communication can obviously relay a positive message just as quickly.

Therefore, have your social media channels ready to quickly blast out an immediate message to combat or apologise for whatever has happened if it's appropriate to do so.

Companies send out letters for product recalls or they'll send people out to repair your tumble dryer that's about to burst into flames. You may even get a voucher for money off your next purchase if a delivered jumper is the wrong colour!

You might need to just reach for a phone to make it more personal. Not everything is going to be a huge disaster.

It's not all bad.

Enough doom and gloom, let's not forget a reputation can be good as well as bad! We just seem to levitate to the negative more so.

Promise number three in the previous chapter, the "Under Promise" is one I highly recommend to employ at any level to begin to nurture a favourable reputation. Under promise to over deliver. To help build my reputation, there's a couple of subtle words I add to my emails to remind my customers that I've done what I said I would do or that I've over delivered. This is just in case they had forgotten the timescales they were expecting.

Instead of "Please find your documents attached." I might add:

"As promised, please find your documents attached."

Or:

"Ahead of schedule, please find your documents attached."

Or:

"A bit earlier than expected, please find your documents attached."

Not world shatteringly insightful, but a little bit of "Nudge" theory in practice.

As much as having your damage limitation strategy ready to go, do have your reputation megaphone equally poised. Promote your success stories through social media platforms. Try to diarise regular blogs and have in mind to create case studies on your website.

In conclusion "be ready", good or bad.

Has that kettle boiled yet?

REPUTATION - STRATEGY QUESTIONS

1. What is your reputation built on? Like your promise, you might start to consider how your messaging is formed by the feedback from your early customers. What is, or are, your "ests"?

2. What actions do you take to consistently build on your reputation? Here I highly recommend strategies for allowing your customers to provide feedback.

3. What is in place to enable other people to pass your products or services on to their friends? Apart from crossing your fingers and hoping customers tell their friends, you could think about all kinds of loyalty schemes for instance.

#4 NAME

HAVE YOU EVER DONE THE VACUUMING?

#4 - A BRAND IS A NAME

In my experience, this is the hardest thing to sort out because it often feels like the most emotional and subjective decision you'll have to make. Although it doesn't have to be - and here are some reasons why that should be the case.

For a moment, try to forget you are starting a business and look at how you act as a consumer. Ask yourself, is there a NAME of a brand that really stops you buying from them? Do you really care that Waitrose is called Waitrose or Flymo is called Flymo or Boots is called Boots? No, you don't. What you really care about is the service, the experience, maybe the price and possibly what that brand stands for.

With that in mind, I will put it to you that your future customers won't really care what you're called either. So the exercise of naming your business doesn't have to be painful or emotionally draining.

Please don't get me wrong, I'm not suggesting you shouldn't care and I'm also not implying that your customers don't need to have a connection with your name. They will, eventually. If we make it easy for them to connect to it as quickly as possible, then that's another element in the branding puzzle that will start earning you money quicker.

The VERY worst thing you can do is to resort to three or more initials based on the names on your birth certificate. It will mean nothing to anyone. It's instantly forgettable. You won't get an exact website domain name and your chances of trademarking it alone are dramatically reduced. Another initialising route I see is when a business decides to call themselves exactly what they do, for example Applied Fuselage Reinforcements, but then shorten it to AFR from day one and think that everyone knows what that means just because they do. That business would then most likely pretend that those three letters are their logo and then promote the three letters really big. Next, they'd have to utilise some space under the three letters to explain what the three letters mean. It's utter madness… but it's number one of the six cornerstones of crap, so it is forgivable!

I know what you're screaming at the book right now…

"What about 'BBC' or 'IBM' or 'B&Q' or 'MFI' then?"

O.K. challenge accepted!

First of all, those initials ARE what you are familiar with, now that these brands are part of the fabric of our society. Those companies have spent millions in marketing to get you to notice them.

Second, they weren't three letters to begin with. They have succumbed to their customers "allowing" them to do so, after the customers shortened them because they were just too much of a mouthful. The British Broadcasting Corporation, Industrial Business Machines, Mallard Furniture Industries and Block & Quayle were all launched as their full names. For example in the case of Block & Quayle the couriers who signed for the deliveries got fed up with writing the name in full and began to shorten it to B&Q.

Thirdly, I've found that the simplicity or difficulty of a business name is directly proportional to how much marketing budget you may have. This book is directed at start-ups and SMEs who tend not to have millions to spend on nightly TV adverts which remind their customers of weird words like "Kodak" or "Zoopla" or "Shpock". So if there's a lack of marketing budget, the business name needs to be able to connect with the target market really quickly when it is seen or heard. If you have no money, the last thing you need to do is make it really difficult for your customers to understand what you do or remember what you're called.

There is still loads of opportunity for creativity. Even if you are called something like Purple Banana which bears no relation to your offering; it still offers us all an instant connection because we understand those words. We have already heard of them, we can recall them and therefore we can pass on to a colleague through word of mouth. Substitute the word "Banana" with the word "Bricks" and you're now hinting at what your offer is - if you were an estate agent for example!

Of course, it's a little more complicated than that for one simple reason: someone's already thought of the name you've come up with!

So here's where RESEARCH is absolutely key. As previously mentioned at the start of the book, 90% of start-ups don't even bother typing their "new" name into a search engine. Why they don't bother eludes me. Perhaps they don't want to be confronted with the idea that what they have come up with isn't original and prefer to pretend. I don't really know. I do understand the disappointment though, it's part and parcel of my everyday life. I can spend hours and hours coming up with names that I think are fantastic, and then spend the next five minutes finding out it's all been done. Nothing's original and for a second I feel completely useless at my job! Luckily that soon goes, as I'm used to it, and I soldier on and get back to the task at hand.

So, how do you come up with an original name I hear you ask? Well, there are plenty of methods I've developed over the years and, of course, the approach will change from one client to the next. There's no quick fix and it does take a certain amount of time to do all the checking and researching. On average it would take me two to three days, so let me try and take some of that pain away for you.

Just like our list of "types of promises" in chapter #2, here's a list of methods that companies have used to come up with their name. As you may have gathered already from my rantings, I'll start with the worst methods and then suggest increasingly better methods.

Naming methods

1. Initials

Not wanting to stereotype market sectors, but stereotypes exist mainly because they're true! You'll find that a lot of trades like plumbers, electricians and decorators will use the initials of their name. Paradoxically they tend to have the least amount of marketing budget but create the hardest company names to remember. Names that tell the customer absolutely nothing about their product or service.

MPW - Plumbing
PRW - Electrics
AMW - Painting and Decorating

The initials tell you nothing. And because they don't, you still have to add the service; and some companies then use up more space to write out the initials in full. A complete waste of time and money. And those W's add three more syllables to the name. Why use five incoherent syllables when you could have less and be more descriptive?

2. Acronyms

The technical difference between initials and acronyms is that acronyms are a sequence of initials that spell out a word. Preferably an existing word that a customer may be familiar with or a new word that can be easily pronounced, based on familiar phonetics.

SCUBA - Self-Contained Underwater Breathing Apparatus
WHO - World Health Organisation
IKEA - Ingvar Kamprad (Founder) lived in Elmtaryd, Agunnaryd.

3. Surname or founder name combinations

Again, stereotyping the markets, but often used by solicitors, estate agents and markets that are known for their partnerships. After that you will see companies named after a surname in most market sectors. However for a start-up or SME with very little marketing budget this will be hard to develop a strong brand. A good reason to use the surname is if the brand is clearly going to be built around the founder.

Marks & Spencer - Michael Marks and Thomas Spencer in 1884
Bass - William Bass in 1777
Pearson, Spectre, Litt - or other real-world law firms!!

4. SEO friendly

This is clearly a recent way of naming companies by people who assume they can be found on the Internet. If you only need to be found online and have no real goal to build a household name - just sell stuff from a website - then this might seem a good way for a customer to find you quickly. This method simply creates a name made up of the words you expect a customer to type into a search engine to find you. The usual drawbacks apply: if you add a geographical word in your name - for growth; or focus on a single product or service - for diversification. And other businesses have probably got there before you. The biggest drawback is that Google state they do not give preference to keyword rich domain names, so it's very much a misinformed approach.

5. Deliberately misspelt

Because most of the useful words in the dictionary have pretty much been taken when it comes to a website domain, the obvious move would be to misspell words. Of course that makes it a lot harder to find online and really boring when you have to constantly tell customers how to spell your name on the phone.

Cazoo - Carfinder company from the word Kazoo
Google - From Googol
Flickr - Losing an "e" became very popular e.g. Tumblr, Whistl and The Weeknd

6. Bricolage - or "tinkering with wordplay"

This covers a few concepts and is a mixture of not quite misspelling but more about being playful, creative or just having to be different because what you actually want is already being used.

a. Vowel substitution
Smoll (not small), **Lyft** (not lift)
b. Consonant substitution
Bratz (dolls), **Qustodian**
c. Spelling backwards
Trebor mints, **Harpo** (productions), **Neerg** Energy
d. Palindromes
AvivA, OxO, CiviC,
e. Onomatopoeia
Hoot, Yahoo, Twitter

f. Anagrams
Gloden (Bristol tanning salon)

7. Puns

I've found it hard to identify strong international brands that are based on puns, which may be a clue as to the integrity of using this method. However, for local businesses, especially hairdressers, it creates a good amount of PR and buzz. It can be memorable and fits certain business personalities. Just be aware of looming lawsuits!

Barber Streisand - Hairdressers
Cod Almighty - Fish and chip shop
Spandau Valet - Car cleaners

8. Completely made up

Häagen-Dazs - Ice cream
Xerox - Photocopiers
Etsy - Vintage e-commerce

9. Single or combos of existing words

I'm sure you'll know many like this. The use of existing words certainly helps a customer instantly connect. Using combinations can help to hint at part of the product, service, benefit, values or personality of the company. However in some cases, none of those applies! The clearest problem with this route is two-fold. The likelihood of someone else already using a very common word before you thought of doing it is extremely high. And the chances of protecting with a trademark is equally unlikely, although not out of the question.

Purple Bricks
The "classic" colour + object combo

Weird Fish
Clothing company that is weirdly not that weird!
Pizza Hut
What you'll eat and where you'll eat it!

10. Portmanteaus or "Word Smash"

I fully admit that I'm putting this at the top because it's my preferred method. However, in my defence, it has produced the best results in terms of originality, availability of domains and the ability to having trademarks granted. The biggest drawback, in my experience, is how hard it is for the client to comprehend the initial unfamiliarity that this creative approach to naming yields. They then place the fear they experience onto their future customers, assuming that customers won't "get it" either. However, if you look at the examples below, you'll see this notion is simply untrue.

This method creates multiple messages to tell the customer what the business is offering. You might combine a specialism with a benefit; or a product with a feature; or similar combinations. You would often use one or two syllables from each word for simplicity to create a new word that is completely original yet still very recognisable, pronounceable and spellable. Sounds easy…? Trust me, it's not!

Netflix
Might just as easily been called "Interfilm" or "Cineweb"
Microsoft
Mr Gates decided not to go for "Tinyware" or "Smalltech"
Pinterest
"Photoboard" or "Hobbywall" were possibly discarded

A further development of word smashing, will be to cut down the syllables even more. I would suggest this isn't as useful to the customer because you will eventually still have to explain what it means. But hey, it might catch on!

Nylon - A combination of **N**ew **Y**ork and **Lon**don
Shpock - As their strapline explains: "a **sh**op in your **pock**et"
Yodel - Claiming to be **yo**ur **del**ivery company.

That's probably not all the methods, but enough to get you thinking, I hope.

Naming suitability checklist

You may be surprised to know, however, that my approach to naming a business is mainly an objective process to begin with. It then filters into other areas to see if it can touch on specialism, differentiating messages, benefits, other existing cultural references and personality.

Just for starters, here are a few objective questions you could (should!) ask yourself when creating a name for a start-up or a company looking for a re-brand. As I mentioned, I start with real objective questions and then filter off into more subjectivity.

Objective criteria - Really needs a YES answer

- Is there a .co.uk or .com available?
- Are other domain extensions available?
- Are there other social media urls available?
- Is there a limited company available for registration?
- Will you be able to trademark it. For starters, no one else has already registered it.
- Does it translate well overseas if you expand?
- Does it need to be found by means other than a search engine?

Subjective criteria - Again best to say YES in most cases, but might need testing.

- Is it differentiating enough?

- Is it memorable or simple to recall?
- Is it easy to spell and are there other ways to spell it?
- Does it sound unique when spoken?
- Does it hint at what the company is offering?
- Could it hint at the personality of the company?
- Will it connect to the right audience?
- Is it non-geographically specific?
- Will it permit future diversification?
- Does it indicate any kind of benefit?
- Are there four syllables or less?
- Can it actually be pronounced easily?

Finally, we kind of answer the chapter heading question because history also tells us that a BRAND is definitely a name, and can even become so synonymous with a product or service that it completely takes over.

We HOOVER around the house (even if we're using a Dyson!). We SELLOTAPE our parcels, we GOOGLE a website. We certainly don't ride a P.W.C. (Personal Water Craft) we ride a Jet Ski. I appreciate you may not be thinking in those terms for your business now, and I can confidently say that the aforementioned companies weren't thinking they would become universal terms for theirs either; or pinched as verbs and nouns on day one of their new business either. However, creating a name using all the reasoning I've suggested will certainly increase the chances of your business name being used as a verb or noun... wouldn't that be great!

NAME - STRATEGY QUESTIONS

1. What is the name of your business/offer/service/product? And have you at least Googled it to see if anyone else is using it or something very similar with other words or spelling.

2. What part of the name informs your audience what your offer is? Or hints at a benefit or creates an impression of personality?

3. Is there any part of your name that could hinder geographical growth or future diversification?

#5 ORIGINAL

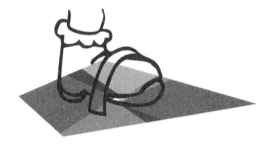

THE SECOND PERSON TO CLIMB EVEREST WAS?

#5 - A BRAND IS ORIGINAL

I don't want to worry you with this element of what makes a great brand. But history shows us that being ORIGINAL, which often suggests being the FIRST in your market, really helps a lot!

Let's take brands like Heinz in 1869 and Coca-Cola in 1886, brands that are still going strong today. Is that due to them being first? Well, when I say Heinz, you're probably thinking of baked beans. But they weren't launched until 1901, and Heinz first started out as Heinz and Noble, and then the longer F & J Heinz Company. They actually launched with a horseradish product and the now famous "ketchup" was launched seven years later, so not an overnight success. Coca-Cola has a similar evolution which notably took them 43 years to finally lose the cocaine! Maybe that's why their product was so good! Perhaps there was very little in the way of competition when they launched. Maybe their marketing budget was superior. As with launching any new business or product, there's literally hundreds of reasons for success or failure. If you're going to be a true pioneer with what you think is a completely original business product or service, then you'll have to take into consideration that these companies also had no idea if anyone needed or wanted their products. Of course, other factors influence the longevity of these companies: investment, determination, drive, even luck!

We went over the brief history of branding in chapter two. You'll remember that, from the 15th century onwards, the biggest influence on branding and getting your message to your customer was with the invention of the printing press. Then in the later 19th century, just as the likes of Heinz and Coca-Cola were blossoming, the industrial revolution was at its peak. This was when it was discovered how to print on all sorts of surfaces, like glass bottles, round tins and many other previously unprintable surfaces. As I've mentioned, William Bass, founder of Bass Brewery, registered the first UK trademark in 1876 and many other businesses followed suit.

Being original was one thing; protecting it, so no one copied you, was quite another! We'll broaden that discussion in our "Value" chapter.

Something borrowed

In whatever year it is as you read this, you're probably thinking everything that could be original has already been thought of. I would suggest that's pretty much the case. But just like the invention of the printing press, seismic shifts in technology can wipe the slate clean and conjure up a whole new set of opportunities to pounce on.

Take Google, Facebook, YouTube and Amazon for example. In the vast history of commerce, very young companies. They all made the best use of the very latest technology at the time and transformed the way customers could search for information, connect with friends, watch videos or buy books. We used to do our research in our local library or ask our parents. We used to meet our mates at Wimpy for a milkshake. We used to record *Top Of The Pops* off our TVs or go to Blockbusters. I got my books (actually mainly comics!) from WH Smith. The modern contemporaries exploited an original way to do something that we already did, but then supposedly offered us improved benefits, like: convenience, speed, price, or choice to ween us off existing methods. I would question, 30-odd years later, whether we have obtained much improved lives because of this technology, but that's another book or rant!

Again, not a topic for this book to discuss, but at the turn of the last century, complete original business models were also being developed by these companies. Apart from Amazon, the other three businesses initially seemed to offer all their services for free! If you suggested that as a model for a business any time before the year 2000, you'd be laughed at for being quite mad, as you clearly had no grasp of the basics of economics. I think we've now learned that if something is free, you're probably the product!

Even these examples of "original" businesses born in the 21st century were helped by their predecessors. We may cite Google as the original search engine, but even I remember the likes of AOL (1985), Yahoo (1994), and Netscape (1994) all doing their best to be number one in the early days, but not quite managing to hold onto market share. Having seen the film *The Social Network*, we now know the concept of online university "facebooks" were part of everyday campus life in America. The likes of Myspace, Friends Reunited and Friendster were all, unbeknownst to them, paving the way for Mr Zuckerberg. YouTube, however, was original in as much as it hosted any video uploaded by anyone in the world. Before that we could stream our own videos on our own computers or on our own websites using digital video player plugins like RealPlayer, QuickTime or Windows Media Player.

As I write this in 2020 (cos I seem to have a lot of time on my hands), the world has changed enormously with ever evolving cultural and ideological mantras to mould into new benefits to satisfy the demand of modern global attitudes. If you're fed up or indeed worried that Google track your every online click then 'Duck Duck Go' or 'Brave' may be the search engine for you. If you've become more socially conscious and wish to support your local bookshop rather than Jeff Bezos (who may or may not still be the CEO of Amazon at the time of publishing!) then buy from bookshop.org. The cycle of life, commerce and offering something "original" continues to evolve.

An original experience

Hopefully, with the above examples we can see that social, economic, technological or cultural shifts, as well as market forces, provide opportunities all the time. You just have to be one of the first to think of turning those opportunities into some sort of a business.

I hear what you're saying (or screaming)! You can't all be first and be completely original. And on balance you'd be right. Most businesses are one of many, offering the same product or service; and who can sit in quite a crowded market.

If you are in such a market I would suggest you ask yourself, *"How can you make the approach to your offer, service or product original?"*. More importantly, *"How original can you make the experience for your customer?"*.

Customers don't comeback because of your name, logo or strapline. These are clearly three very important aspects to establish your brand, but your customers will consistently come back if they've had a great experience. That great experience, as we've mentioned previously, would often be passed on to friends and colleagues by word of mouth.

One simple strategy that I suggest to start-ups, or reasonably young businesses, is to first of all try to find out what your competitors are doing wrong and "simply" concentrate on doing that thing right. We can often recall hearing stories of entrepreneurs remarking that they *"needed something that did something and couldn't find exactly what they wanted"* so they invented that missing "something" themselves. As I write this I came across an advert for a new type of belt called the GRIP6. The inventor was fed up with existing buckles being too bulky, annoyed you couldn't interchange the buckles and didn't like the way the end flappy bit "flapped". So they just changed everything. The humble belt we were all seemingly happy with for hundreds of years changed overnight. The company has also ploughed into the sock market!

Just think of the incremental evolution of serving a cup of coffee, pushing a baby in a perambulator or making a phone call! I'm sure you can think of everyday items, products or services that you like because they offer something better now than they did before. If you ever find yourself fed up with something and wish it was different, then you may have stumbled across a business opportunity. Not forgetting that just because you've found a "gap in the market", make sure there's a "market in that gap".

The original "holy triumvirate"

The next chapter is about "difference", and you may want to argue that in some cases being "original" is another variation on just being different. Is a non-bulky buckle compared to a bulky buckle something original or something different? Is a unique selling point actually completely unique? In my experience, not really. It depends on how you market or promote your point of difference.

The building blocks discussed so far are very much, thoughts, philosophies and amorphous manifestations of your business ideas. It's at this point, when discussing originality, we need to think about "graphically representing" those concepts. Just so you know, I'll use this phrase a lot. The "holy triumvirate" in my game is the "Name", "Logo" and "Strapline" and this is the beginning of transforming all your business's passions and promises into text and images so as to engage customers when you can't be in front of them or on a phone having a chat.

Name

There is a whole chapter dedicated to this, because it is an essential building block which can start to engage the audience you want to attract. So these are just a few words to highlight the initial importance of trying to convey as much originality or scarcity as you can.

Whilst writing this book I had the wonderful experience of being "quoted" for the very first time by a recent customer of mine. It was a baby ultrasound scanning clinic, and in our very first meeting I apparently said:

"People tend not to accept originality because they've never seen it."

It was something that stuck with him and I'll certainly be dining out on that for some time! My newly acquired infamy aside, this attitude to being original is a massive obstacle for making a business stand out.

I know this because of the many, many times I've been asked to come up with an original company name. A name would then be rejected for the very fact that the client had never heard of it before, even though they asked for something original. I expand on this in the "naming" chapter, by pointing out that Microsoft, Netflix or Pinterest are all completely original names that didn't exist before they were made up. Even as you are reading this I know, with a certain degree of confidence, that you are completely at ease with those business names. You have at some point engaged or acknowledge those names and you have completely accepted them as if they couldn't be called anything else. I therefore confidently suggest, if you came up with an original name your customers will be just as accepting straight away. It's not easy to be original, but it's possible and if you use my favourite method of word smashing, just like "Netflix", it can be done.

Logo

Once you've got your name and you've bought the domain and done all the research to make sure no one else has got it, you'll need an original looking logo. Now this isn't easy. After all, that's my job and I've spent over 25 years perfecting how to do it. As the owner of your business you should be able to develop and control all the building blocks that are being discussed in this book. Unless you're starting up a graphic design business, I would urge you to outsource to a professional to help you out with your logo.

You may be surprised to notice that I haven't got a chapter on logos. That's because it may need a whole book in itself. It's also very deliberate, because it's the one element that confuses most people who think your logo is your brand. I will, however, look at logos a little more broadly in the next chapter as it's really, really hard to have an original logo; but having one that's different is a little easier.

Strapline

Then finally in the holy triumvirate, an original "strapline". Again, there's a good reason why I've written a whole chapter on this and also started laying the initial thoughts around this in the "promise" chapter. I can hear myself going on, so forgive me, but this is so important to get right. I'll repeat myself again, branding is "the promise to your customer". So your strapline should be starting to reflect or encompass some, if not all, of that promise. You can jump to the "strapline" chapter if you want now and I'll see you back here in 15 minutes!

If these initial three tangible graphical representations of your brand can have some originality about them they will help enormously when trying to attract the right customers as well as set you apart from your competition.

Originality is scarce and scarcity is valuable and we'll summarise the element of value in a later chapter. Meanwhile, we need to expand on other graphical representations of a brand which are very hard to be completely original, so let's move on to being "different".

Who was the second person to climb Everest? I've no idea!

ORIGINAL - STRATEGY QUESTIONS

1. What aspect of your service or product can become original?

2. What original experiences can you offer your customer?

3. Is your name, logo or strapline original and can you protect them? If you do nothing at all, please Google your name ideas before you start getting shop signs done. The last thing you need is to get sued or shut down for not being original.

#6 DIFFERENT

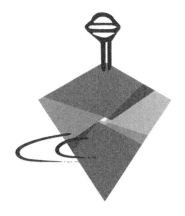

SING A DIFFERENT TUNE
#6 - A BRAND IS DIFFERENT

Moving on from the last chapter, we have to eventually conclude: if you can't be ORIGINAL then you should at least be DIFFERENT. Alas, not only have I come across many a business's fear of being original, but there have been plenty who have been equally scared of being different.

If you can't be original or different then you may be forced down the route of being the cheapest, which doesn't bode well. You may notice BRANDED products are almost never the cheapest. They offer the customer VALUE in other ways, like shared passions, better promises or a stronger reputation.

After well over 25 years of advising on branding, I still haven't found one good reason for blending in with your competition and hiding yourself away from your customers.

But, businesses do it all the time.

I've tried to help businesses that offer replica products or services as others in their market, say an insurance company, for instance.

They have said to me, *"We've seen that a lot of our competitors have blue logos, so we think we should have the same, as that's obviously the colour for our market."*.

Audible sigh...

Now if I say to you, even though there are many supermarkets to choose from, which one is orange? You'd hopefully say Sainsbury's. Despite the literally over-saturated market of chocolate bars, who makes the purple ones? Cadbury, of course. Being different, in whatever way you can, is clearly helpful.

If your service or product, in all intents and purposes, is identical to someone else, the ONE thing you really should do is make it look different, stand out from the crowd, grab your customers' attention.

Give your customers the chance to not only find you in a sea of mediocrity, but also give them a chance to remember you and pass on your difference to their friends.

I mentioned I'd expand on logos in this chapter, because creating an original one is quite difficult. I'll start the "different" campaign by steering you clear of some minefields that businesses seem to enter all the time. Like the aforementioned, *"our market is blue"*, there are obvious reasons why people make simple mistakes over and over, and they are all in the "six cornerstones of crap". Fear is the biggest one. For the same reasons a lot of tradespeople just use their initials for their company name, they also use the same logo as their competitors.

Let me demonstrate! Plumbers and heating engineers use half a flame and half a water droplet. Estate agents use a whole house. Roofers use the top half of a house, especially if their name starts with an "A". Painters and decorators use a paintbrush and a house. Electricians use a bulb or a flash of lightening. A vast amount of businesses, no matter what market, use a swish or arc of some kind. I could "vent" for another two hours but I'll stop there!

If you've noticed the logo examples, you might be amazed at, not just the similarity but, the identical-ness (if that's a word?) of them. I'm not!

So what kind of wisdom can I impart so you don't make the same mistakes? I've already suggested you engage a professional logo designer, and moreover, a branding consultant for one special reason… they actually do think DIFFERENTLY.

More specifically, my take on "different thinking" can be broken down into:

1. **Divergent thinking** - The imagining of all possibilities that exist and don't necessarily exist yet!
2. **Associative thinking** - Exploring connections between those possibilities and seemingly unrelated ideas.
3. **Convergent thinking** - The discernment of what would be the best choice, once a selection of ideas are in front of you.

On top of that, and I'm not kidding, it helps if us "creatives" are dyslexic! We literally see words and numbers differently to most people. Often I see an anagram of a word before I see the actual word in front of me. This particular "defect" helps me come up with new names more easily than someone who can only see, understand and accept words that are spelt or pronounced "correctly".

If you haven't heard of, or read about "The Paperclip Experiment" then do check it out, as it will explain a lot of what I'm describing here. Unfortunately, rightly or wrongly standard schools educate creativity out of most of us. In the pursuit of being taught the "right" or "accepted" answers to most questions in a test, we eventually stop needing to think differently and just repeat the same answers the previous years were taught. If you're lucky you may get to question your tutor once you get to university. But for 98% of us, it's too late.

Look up George Land's and Beth Jarman's Paperclip Experiment, it's fascinating and a little saddening at the same time!

Let's take coming up with a logo for an estate agent. 98% of adults will suggest a house is the only solution. There are three reasons why they come up with that as an answer:

1. Because it's the "right" answer. Estate agents sell houses, end of!
2. All they can see is other estate agent logos which are houses, which therefore reinforces their initial belief.
3. The part of their brain that used to think divergently has been shut down, leaving only the convergent part to recognise what's "right" as quick as it can.

Most adult brains quickly engage the convergent part of the brain too quickly. Even if some part of the divergent brain is desperately trying to think "outside of the box", the convergent part is simultaneously dismissing alternative ideas before they've even had the chance to be tested out.

Let me quickly demonstrate how my brain would look at coming up with an estate agency logo. You may then see a different method of coming up with other ideas for other projects or businesses.

STEP 1: Divergent thinking

Initially, I break down this thought process into two distinct areas:

1. What product and/or service is being offered by the estate agent?

97

2. What about the product and / or service benefits the customer?

There's only one rule here: Don't engage your convergent brain, nothing is a bad idea... yet! I promise you I'll do this right now with no preparation!

PRODUCT – What else is closely related to a house?

House - Windows - Doors - Chimney - Roof - Aerial - Satellite Dish - Tiles - Gutter - Slate - Bricks - Mortar - Driveway - Fence - Number - Letterbox - Road name sign - Post code - Rooms - Garden - Grass - Flowers - Bees - Birds

SERVICE – Can you break down all the elements of an estate agent?

Buying - Selling - Advertising - Window displays - Mortgage advice - Surveys - Showing you round - For Sale sign - Finance - Documentation - Market portals

BENEFITS – List as many benefits to the customer as you can.

Peace of mind - Experience - Professional - Safe pair of hands - Tradition - Heritage - Knowledge - Speed - Guarantees - Money off - No stamp duty - No VAT - Local - Friendly - Team of contractors - Recommended partner professions - Security

STEP 2: Associative thinking

This is where the "paperclip" thinking comes in, and I'd ask myself what else can I connect with the words that we've come up with?

House:

Apartment - Flat - Shack - Bedsit - Detached - Terrace -
Digs - Abode - Mansion - Castle - Keep - Lighthouse - Igloo
- Den - Drey - Nest - Sty - Hive - Web - Holt - Coop - Roost
- Kennel - Aviary - Cage - Crib

Living in house:

Family - Growing up - Happy memories - Swing -
Slide - Paddling pool - Pond - Mowing the lawn - Pets -
Good times/sad times - Pencil marks on the kitchen
wall for children's heights - Bunk beds - Sharing your
room with a sibling - Dad's shed - Potting shed -
Planting flowers - Growing your own veg - Hanging
out the washing - Mending the car - Washing the car -
First day of school - Neighbours

STEP 3: Convergent thinking

As you're now aware, this is where I'd sift through the ideas.
I'll probably see if there are more links between steps one and
two first before I start dismissing stuff. In this quick exercise I
notice that in step one we see the word "bird" and in step two
we see the word "nest". It's these little links that I'll then
explore and start sketching out to begin the actual process of
coming up with a logo.

Hopefully that was useful. This process can help you move
past the obvious straight away and open up other
possibilities. Not forgetting you can go to the extreme and
come up with anything if you have the marketing clout
behind it. Here in Bristol there is an estate agent simply called
Elephant with, unsurprisingly, a simple graphic of an
elephant's trunk with an eye. I'd be interested in the story
behind it, but it doesn't matter. It's different from anything
else in Bristol, where there are over 400 types of sales, lettings
and property management agents. It does the job.

Engage a different brain

I would suggest that the primary selling point and the best reason to work with a creative/designer, is that their brain will think differently than yours. Crucially they should be able to come up with a logo that can be protected by trademark because it will be markedly different from competitors in the same market.

We'll discuss this further in the "Value" chapter. Suffice to say that if your differences can be protected, your brand and your business will increase in value.

Creatives will think divergently for a long period of time (literally days at a time) where nothing will be deemed wrong or right. Then their brains can move on to the convergent task of weighing up the pros and cons of all the ideas and start to narrow them down until the most appropriate idea or choice of ideas is left.

Having read the "cornerstones of crap" chapter, you now know there's still a possibility you may not choose the absolute best option. The creative should be able to tell you which is the best choice. I'll leave that with you. Alternatively, ask yourself: *"Why would you pay someone to do 90% of their job and then get you to do the last 10%?"*.

To me it's like going to a doctor, asking them to diagnose a problem you have and they know exactly how to help you. In this analogy, instead of prescribing the bottle of pills that will make you better, they offer four bottles and leave it for you to decide which one to take.

I'm certainly not here to put "creatives" out of a job, but now that I've explained how it's possible to think differently, you may be better placed to come up with a logo that's not the same as your competitors.

Different is valuable

Some may argue (and many have!) that surely it's best to be the same or similar to what's gone before because people like familiarity. They are comfortable and trust things that aren't too different. I agree with some of that sentiment in other contexts. Some scrupulous businesses absolutely rely on that impulse with undiscerning consumers. The counterfeit market is worth around £14 billion (2016) on UK imports alone. The biggest enabler of this fraudulent trade is hoping that the punters see a very familiar looking logo and think it's the real thing. Combinations of similar colours, typefaces and graphics all help with the illusion. Admittedly, this level of completely copying the graphical representation of a well-known brand is not how most businesses operate. An important distinction here is that this practice is not about similar businesses operating in a competitive market. It's plain criminality. Legitimate businesses have the law on their side to try and stop it happening.

Camouflage rackets

In a murkier legal area, there are more devious (or outrageous) ways a new or even established market competitor will trade off another brand's goodwill to attract business. In legal terms it's called "passing off". In layman's terms we'd call it "ripping off"! This practice will deliberately use a slight adaption of a competitor's colours, typefaces and supporting graphics because they know that consumers will transfer the goodwill without too much fuss and buy from them.

Supermarkets are notorious for tapping into this trusting behaviour. They, like me, know how much the role of strong branding determines people's shopping habits; and how loyal they become to simple things like a combination of graphics, images, colours and typefaces. Saying that out loud does sound like my profession is incredibly manipulative and evil, but if I can be allowed to proceed... It's not the process or use of branding that's manipulative, it's incredibly useful and helpful to the business and consumer. It does however open up possibilities of a rival company copying a competitive brand to trick customers into buying theirs. Like many practices in commerce, opportunists will find short cuts to make a quick buck.

Three things hit me when I see the examples of these copycats. Firstly, I can't quite believe the gall of the pretenders who even thought it was a good idea to masquerade as their competitors. Secondly, it amazes me how, in some cases, they actually get away with it, with no legal intervention. Lastly, and because there is clear evidence that these companies sometimes get away with it, maybe it is a good strategy after all? That is a fleeting thought though! Taking risks in business is always something you have to consider. And maybe at some level this is a risk worth taking for some businesses. Perhaps the cost of a court case is actually cheaper than the advertising, marketing and PR that they get for free in the public legal battle.

ASDA's Puffin vs the McVitie's Penguin, in my opinion, was a clear "rip-off". They even copied the strapline for "Pick up a Puffin". No wonder McVitie's won their claim of "passing-off". Tesco's 'Puffin' didn't seem to worry McVitie's and Morrison's 'Toucan' just wasn't worth the fuss. Data from studies have shown that up to 20% of sales can be lost from a brand leader to the copycat. So, McVitie's were going to do all they could to hang on to the whole £30 million they got from that one product alone. More recently, Poundland thought they could "get away" with introducing their Twin Peaks chocolate bar, claiming as they did, it in no way resembled Mondelēz's Toblerone. They were soon made to change their packaging and to re-mould their bars more accurately to the English mountains they originally claimed were the inspiration. Utter twaddle!!!

'Twin Peaks' before and after, plus original Toblerone.

More crafty copy cats doing their best to fool the public!

I suspect that you're not a business the size of Prada, Chanel, McVitie's or Walkers (yet). So you probably don't have to worry about people fraudulently copying your branded products. At the smaller scale of owning a local or regional business, you can force your competitors who are "chancing their arm" with similar branding to yours to cease and desist if you have a trademark or can prove the that the passing off is clearly confusing the market. In essence my argument to be "different" is quite plain and simple. Firstly to protect your business and secondly, I'm sorry to say it, to stand out! Don't be scared, it's going to be fine!

Difference is helpful

So far we've covered getting an original name and strapline and have just nailed how easy it is to get an extremely different looking logo. As shown in the few examples previously. We now have a few more elements within the graphical representation of a brand that we should look at to create a difference:

1. Colour scheme
2. Typefaces
3. Imagery: photography/illustrations/drawings/paintings/cartoons
4. Product design (shape and form)
5. Other supporting graphics
6. Advertising and marketing collateral concepts

Colour

As my dentist will attest, I have a love of chocolate. And I have always taken an interest in the many different wrappers to the point of collecting them as a kid. Double Deckers were my favourite for some reason, and I literally had hundreds and hundreds of them. I now have five crowns and fillings in all teeth bar my four front ones! I can see now that whatever I found fascinating at the time, spilled over to my lineage from graphic designer to branding consultant. The differences across the products could be distilled into the above list.

I mentioned before that we instinctively know that a purple bar of chocolate is highly likely to be made by Cadbury. Actually the chances are 100%, because Cadbury had even protected, by trademark, a specific shade of purple that no one else can use. That's how serious these companies are about protecting their difference. They had that protection for a good 24 years, but due to a slight oversight they limited the colour to tablet shaped bars. When they wanted to transfer the protection to other non-tablet shaped products, they were challenged and lost their case. However, I'm merely pointing out that this demonstrates my initial argument against companies saying they should be blue because everyone else in their market is. This is simply not true and just plain nonsense when it comes to making strategic business and brand decisions early on.

Heinz have also trademarked the specific turquoise colour on their baked bean cans. Christian Louboutin's distinctive red, as used on the soles of its shoes, is also protected. When I say protected, it's quite a narrow protection limited to a certain description and stops very close competitors in the exact same market from copying. It's not that these colours can't be used by anyone else in other commercial sectors. There are others: Tiffany's Blue (which is actually a shade lighter than Heinz's!); T-Mobile's Magenta; UPS's Brown; Barbie's Pink; 3M's Canary Yellow for their Post-it product line. I could go on, but hopefully I'm making my point. Being different and protecting your differences is a valuable and worthwhile pursuit. I'll talk more about the ins and outs and costs of protecting your difference through trademarking in the "value" chapter.

I am including you in this: like it or not, consumers will buy on packaging alone. Loyal customers of Coca-Cola are drawn to the colours, the traditional sign written typeface, the shape of the glass bottle and the lifestyle messaging of the adverts. But they will choose Pepsi as a better tasting product in a blind taste test.

O.K. we branding consultants are slightly evil!

Name, logo and strapline aside; if your colours, typefaces or even shape of product has no distinguishing difference to your competitors, you've already made your task of developing loyal customers much harder than is necessary. I take this approach at the start of the process when choosing the name. Why make it difficult for your customers to initially find you… Then remember you… And lastly recall you from memory to tell their friends? The same thought process is best applied to every aspect of your graphical packaging as well. If you stand out more, you'll embed quicker and deeper into the memory of your customers. I'll try not to harp on in too much depth, this is supposed to be a quick read to get some concrete tips and we've only just covered colour.

Typefaces

First of all, I've got to sort out one little gripe of mine, and in so doing give you the chance to show off! People say "font" when they actually mean "typeface" and here's the proper difference:

Helvetica, Times, Comic Sans, and Calibri are different "typefaces".

Helvetica **Bold**, Times *Italic*, Comic Sans Regular and Calibri Light are different "fonts" or "weights" from within their typeface family.

Helvetica Bold is therefore a font variant of the Helvetica typeface family. Helvetica itself is not a font.

107

Petty I know, but consider yourself well informed. When I've pointed this out people think I'm a dick, so use this information cautiously!

Using typefaces as an example here really helps cement why we use the phrase "graphical representation". If we take your business name… Which happens to also be a word that can be found in a dictionary… And you type it out using a very standard typeface chosen from the list on your computer… Nothing can be protected. So we think of ways we can graphically represent that word to create differences; even original elements if possible.

1. Choose a non-standard typeface that's not one supplied on your computer. Go to a typeface website like myfonts.com
2. Do something to slightly change a letter within the chosen typeface
3. Maybe don't use a capital letter at the start of the word
4. Maybe use all capitals
5. Use more than one colour within the letters
6. Reverse the letters out of a shape (rectangle, oval, lozenge etc.)

Harrods, Nickelodeon, Nutella, Vogue, eBay and Marvel *could* then be "graphically represented" like this…

Harrods nickelodeon

nutella VOGUE

ebay MARVEL

Oh, they already are!!

And to be clear, these are not "logos" but can be referred to as "wordmarks" or "logotypes". What they definitely can be called are "marks" that represent the business's "trade". This is because these representations are now significantly different from when they were just words typed on a keyboard using a standard typeface that everyone has access to. Clearly this is why we have the word "trademark". If you look up the definition of "Mark" you'll read:

1. A small area on a surface having a different colour from its surroundings.
2. A line, figure, or symbol made as an indication or record of something
3. Write a word or symbol on (an object) in order to give information.

Which pretty much describes the above logotypes, especially when they are placed on an object in order to give a customer the information as to what brand they are buying.

———

Imagery

As the "difference" list shows, I've split "imagery" into several options. Let's look at photography first as that's the most accessible - pretty much every one of us is equipped with a camera in the form of a smartphone these days. Although this clearly doesn't make us all photographers!

Imagery tends to start becoming part of the graphical representation of your brand when you start thinking about marketing your brand. You'll need photos on your website, your flyers, your social media posts and blogs. If business cards still exist when this book is published, you might have a photo of yourself on that.

A bit of advice, don't use library shots. It's tempting, but here's the problem. You'll spot a shot that looks really good (and that's already taken half an hour of your valuable time). It's perfect, it sums up your business, it's got all the elements you need. Well guess what, it's so perfect that it also suits your competitor's business as well. That's why it's already been downloaded 17,547 times!

Secondly, people now inherently or sub-consciously know a library shot when they see it. Because of that, it says nothing, it doesn't actually add to your brand or story or difference. It's bland, it's a filler.

Thirdly, it's quite a myth to think it's cheaper than original photography. At the time of writing this book there are several well-known image/photo library platforms: Shutterstock, iStock, Alamy, and many more. There's also a wide range of quality. A decent photo will cost in the region of £20-£80. One photo at £20 might sound O.K., but what about five or ten? You can hire a professional photographer for a day to take 20 photos for £200 - £400 and get the exact shots you want. Obviously, I'm talking within reason here. They won't be taking shots in the Bahamas. A day at your office or factory, or a studio shoot of your products will provide the right story. It will be original, your competitors won't have the same shots and it could actually be cheaper than library shots. You just need to plan and make the most of the photographer's time.

It might be too early in the vision for your brand, but when taking these photos you can start thinking about the style of the shots. Just like the differences I've suggested you can make with typed words, you can implement that with your photography.

1. Black and white only
2. Black and white with just one accent colour
3. Other monotone or duotone colouring to reflect the brand colours
4. Short depth of field
5. High contrast

And so on.

Sometimes a brand can be simply identified by the style of their photography, like Calvin Klein's black and white hunk & waif look; or the classic mouth-wateringly rich M&S food shots. This would also be more obvious with the moving image in TV advertising as well.

Adding alternative imagery to photos - like illustrations, diagrams or cartoons - actually broadens your chances of being different. The artist, cartoonist or technical drawer who you commission, will have their own inherent style, which they hopefully haven't offered to a competitor. You'll already know and instantly recognise many products just because of the illustrations or cartoons associated with the packaging: Tony the Tiger on Frosties; the kilted shot putter of Scott's Porridge Oats; the Jolly Green Giant on a can of sweetcorn. Captain Birdseye on a packet of fish fingers. The penguin on... (not to be confused with a puffin!) a Penguin chocolate bar! I'm sure you can think of many more.

Product shape

I will keep going with the confectionary theme here, as they really do provide us with great examples of how you can still create difference within such a crowded market. Probably because of necessity to stand out, the chocolate bars themselves come in all manner of shapes and sizes, all adding to yet another level of difference. We've already discussed Mondelēz's Toblerone and its uniquely ridged bar. But there are many more that you can recognise purely by the shape and chocolate application without any packaging or graphics.

For a little quiz, just look at the examples and see how many you can identify?

Of course there are many other industries that place a lot of importance on shape design to give their customers help with identifying their product. Just to test an extreme, take the automotive industry for their array of shaped products: VW's Beetle; (originally) British Leyland's Mini, (now owned by BMW); Jaguar's E-Type; the Jeep; the Morris Minor and so on. I must admit cars were a little easier to distinguish back in the days when they had character. The more that design has concentrated on streamline efficiency, the harder it's become to distinguish. The variety in perfume bottles is another big area where the shape of product plays a big part in differentiation. I appreciate that If you're a service-lead business, the last few paragraphs haven't helped. So let's discuss another couple of ways to make you stand out.

Supporting graphics

You could say that an image/photo/cartoon could be placed under the banner of "supporting graphic", but let's get a little more specific. Supporting graphics or "brand assets", can or should help your audience recognise your brand - even when the name, logo and strapline aren't visible within your marketing collateral. These "supporting graphics" may take the form of an extra "swish" or "block" of colour used on an advert perhaps. Or a textured paper or other material look on the back of a letterhead maybe. Or potentially a repeated graphical pattern displayed on some packaging.

Here is a demonstration of a brand that we developed to show these 'supporting graphics' in action. Name, logo and strapline to begin with and then other elements we'll then use within the marketing collateral.

 Picture perfect peace of mind

Above: Name, Logo and Strapline. Below: Supporting graphics

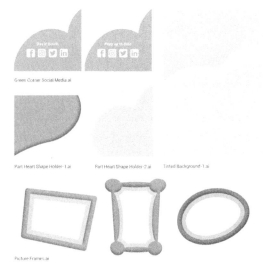

114

A5 Leaflet - Front

A5 Leaflet - Back

Clinic internal wallpaper #1 - Brislington

Supporting graphics (brand assets) now 'in action' within marketing collateral

You'll find that these assets will gradually become part of the representation of your brand, as and when you start to create or commission the design of supporting marketing collateral. Once you decide on doing some marketing, you'll soon realise that you'll need more than your name, logo and strapline to play with. I have said on occasion to my clients that we make sure we design a logo that "works hard for you". By that I'd mean that we would consider blowing the logo up and taking sections of it to use within the marketing. This is a good test to know whether the design of your logo had some distinctive features in the first place. If you can take a section of it and it's still recognisable, then it's passed the test, and is a logo that has the ability to "work hard for you". Talking of marketing collateral, what else can we do to grab your audience's attention?

Marketing collateral

I did say previously that those of you who are offering a service rather than a product would have found that providing a differentiating "shape" would be difficult. Well here's where you can make up for that: when it comes to marketing yourself! The last of our six areas to make a difference is the very first one with which your prospective customers will actually engage with: your brand's graphical representation in all its glory! You've got your name, logo and strapline. Your photos are sorted, you've commissioned a cartoon mascot with an enigmatic smile, and you're quite pleased with that brushed aluminium swish you'll be using somewhere. Your arsenal of assets are at your disposal to now get a graphic designer to come up with a double sided A5 leaflet.

STOP!!! Let's not fall at the last hurdle.

How many A5 leaflets come through your letterbox every week? Can you really cast your mind back and distinguish between any of them? How many do you think you've thrown in the bin in the past year? The harsh truth is your prospective customers are going to do exactly the same.

Here's where you can make yet another difference and chip away at that "gap" where only you will belong and that you will own eventually.

My point being, is that there are different shapes other than A5, A4 or even A6 postcards. Squares, circles, ovals, hexagons, triangles, bespoke shapes, even paper engineering with pop-up sections. Why stop there? You don't have to always print on paper. What about wood, metal, vinyl, foil, fabric, stone, transparent material, rubber and so on.

Then again, you don't even have to "print". You could etch, engrave, crochet, knit, spray, bake, mould, stick. I've done a few of them!

Hopefully you get my gist. Think differently! It will help, I promise.

I know what you're going to say: *"Won't all that cost more?"*, and yes, of course it will! I didn't say being different was the cheap option. Although that said, if your differentiated leaflet yields more profitable results than the generic one, then it may turn out to be very "cheap" indeed. Here I'm talking about return on investment (R.O.I.) which is another strong element to consider and track within your marketing strategy.

But here I have just picked on one type of basic off-line marketing that most start-ups try out. Of course there are many, many ways to market yourself: off, on, above and below the "line". Alas, this book is about the building blocks of branding. I'm afraid you're going to have to get a different book for your marketing strategies!

I think that's sufficiently enough to say about being different.

Onward!

DIFFERENT - STRATEGY QUESTIONS

1. If you're offering an identical product or service to others, what can you do to look different?

2. What different reasons, other than price, can you give your customers to buy INTO you, rather than just FROM you.

3. What messages and experiences can be made different from your competitors?

#7 APPROPRIATE

CHEAP AS CHIPS

#7 - A BRAND IS APPROPRIATE

Unless I suddenly think of something part way through writing this chapter, this won't be as long as the previous heavy hitters! Being appropriate is essentially quite easy. You simply need to look like your price point!

It's one of the starting points of "positioning" in your market, and we'll touch on other measures of positioning later on. Put simply are you "Cheap and cheerful", "Reassuringly expensive" (as a well-known BRAND suggests) or somewhere in between?

"Looking" like your price point is achieved in many ways, and should have already started with your company name and logo, and possibly your strapline if you've decided to go for one. I've re-branded many one-man-bands because they simply looked and sounded like a small business. Purely because of the unimaginative name of their business, it appeared that they couldn't provide a sufficient service to their target market. The owners wanted to take on better paid work and/or bigger clients, but their existing branding wasn't "appropriate" in the eyes of the customers they were trying to attract. So they couldn't move past their price point with the branding they had.

So be mindful of what your vision is. Try not to think of what you are at the start of your business journey. Try to have an idea of what you want your business to be, say in three to five years' time. As the saying goes: "Dress for the job you want, not the one you have". If you plan to look like what you wish to be in the future, you are more likely to get there quicker. The chapter on "Perception" deals with this notion.

In terms of what you may call your company, think very carefully about whether you want to use your given birth name or surname. A complaint that I often get when a business first comes to us three to five years into trading is that customers often ask for the owner by name. They come to us for a brand re-fresh because the owner was what the brand was built around in the early days. Sometimes it can be a struggle to grow if your customers don't trust anyone else in the company, and you can't bring other managers up through the business to take on your role. Get the name appropriate for your five-year strategy in the first place and your customers will buy into the overall philosophy of the business rather than the owner. This tends to make life a little easier in the long term.

Appropriate name and offering

Two other things to consider early on with the name in relation to a long-term strategy is not being too specific about your location or your specific services or products. When I started talking to businesses about branding, the idea of being massively successful wasn't at the forefront of their minds. That has changed a lot lately, where young start-ups seem to think they'll be millionaires before they're thirty. I whole heartily applaud this, although the statistic of companies failing in the first five years hasn't changed in all that time!

I mention this because of the instances when businesses add their location to their name, like "Bristol" or "South West" for instance. Suddenly, because they didn't have a specific vision, they unwittingly become successful and get an opportunity to open up another office in Swindon or Reading a few years down the line. At this point, it might not be "appropriate" to have the word "Bristol" in a business name - because it may hinder your growth plans to go national.

The other hinderance about the appropriateness of a company name is including a word that describes the one service or product you have decided to build your business on. Earlier in this book, within the top ten research questions, I asked: *"Can you diversify or expand your product or service?"* Ask yourself this while coming up with your business name. You might be really focused on selling cupcakes right now. But will calling yourself "Betty's Cup Cakes" stop you selling wedding cakes in the future? On the one hand, marketeers (quite rightly) suggest to focus and niche a business, especially when it comes to messaging and targeting an audience. But on the other, sometimes being a little more generic on a business name allows for easier future expansion.

Appropriate collateral

The much bigger area of your brand's appropriateness is how you are graphically packaging yourself through your marketing collateral.

Before they buy from you, your prospective customers will have seen your marketing. Be that from the look of your website, or a leaflet through the post or an advert on a bus. They will notice the design, the quality of photography, even the thickness of the printed paper, and they will subconsciously or consciously compare all that with the price of your product. Combined with your collateral and how it's presented along with any experience of your competitors, is where they will decide whether your proposition or offer is appropriate or not. Ultimately the price will be either too expensive, suspiciously cheap or just about right.

In the most part, well-known brands are more expensive and small businesses don't think "branding" is for them: "*It's for the likes of Apple and Pepsi.*", they would exclaim. There are plenty of brands out there well known for their cheapness, i.e. Poundland or Lidl. And when Lidl started to look like M&S with their Christmas campaigns, it looked a "Lidl inappropriate".

If you're in the business of selling really cheap products then all I'm suggesting is: don't spend too much on foil blocking on your business card or getting David Bailey to do your photoshoot. Alternatively if you feel like starting up an exclusive luxury car business demanding a minimum of £100K, you will have to spend more than £10 on a brochure and refrain from knocking up your own templated website to entice your customers.

The marketing of your BRAND IMAGE just needs to look like your price point. There's no right or wrong, there's just appropriate. The ultimate trick is to come in just under what you look like.

Appropriate positioning

Actually I have thought of a few more things. So this chapter might be a bit longer than I originally thought!

The first thing "positioning" makes me think of is my last class of juniors before going to "big' school". I think we can all take ourselves back to those days and pretty much nail our "position" in class against 30 or so other competitors in quite a tight "market". We could measure ourselves against "coolness", "likeableness", "sportiness" or '"bookwormyness"!! Whatever it was, we kind of knew where we stood. Where our place was.

I've banged on about the price point, as that's usually the first reference point that your customers will assess you on in relation to your immediate competitors. However, there are many other gauges that you can be measured on, which determine your position in your particular market. Imagine your market as a graph with an X and a Y axis in the middle of a box (see graph below). Let's say that the Y axis (vertical) is price and would range from most expensive at the top to cheapest at the bottom. We can then place a different attribute to your offering along the X axis (horizontal). Take "quality" for instance. You then measure yourself against competitive offerings and their quality against their price. Yes, you'd expect a high quality offering to have a high price and vice versa, but there's always room for manoeuvre. That is exactly how you will be jostling for your position. You can then attribute all kinds of measurements if "quality" doesn't help. "healthy", "speed", "environmentally friendly", "family orientated", "weight", "size" and so on.

Here is your 'position' in the market based on price and quality.

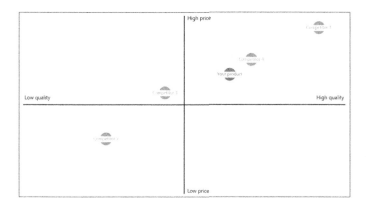

Yes, I'm going to use chocolate as an example again!

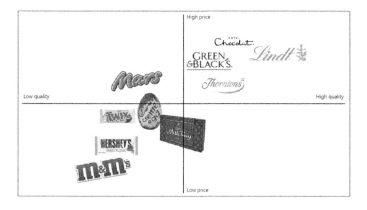

Your sole job, through consistent messaging (we'll get on to that in another chapter), is to make sure your target market knows that you own that space and you are the only brand that has your particular combination of measurements (i.e. a certain price for a certain quality with a certain level of eco credentials).

At the age of ten in class 5a, I held the unique position of "great at cartoons, O.K. in goal, useless at top trumps". I knew my place!

Once you've narrowed down your particular position, one small tip would be to make sure you keep track of what's going on around you as time goes on. Evaluate your price point on a regular basis. You're probably going to invest in different areas of your business overtime which may affect your initial position parameters like quality or speed or level of tech etc. If those parameters change you'll need to inform your customers. Of course new competitors will always be entering your market jostling for position. So you might have to go into the playground after school and get a little aggressive!

Appropriate extensions and alliances

When you're building your brand, you're building many other intentions along the way. Some of which are chapter titles in this book. You're appropriateness gives your customers a perception, which in turn builds your reputation, hopefully in a good way. You're building a connection with your target audience and in turn they are hopefully building an allegiance to you and are buying into your proposition. So it might not be appropriate to suddenly sell something cheap when it's been selling at a higher price. Sometimes a business's "exclusive" pricing is what keeps a customer's loyalty. The reverse is clearly true as well. Putting your prices up may be inappropriate if the perceived value doesn't go up in line with the price hike. Suddenly giving discounts or having sales might not be appropriate. We might all be a bit freaked out if DFS didn't have a sale! This is why you really need to get the price point right to begin with, and make sure you are comfortable with the value of your offering at that price. If no one's buying and you slash prices, you are immediately devaluing yourself and that's not a good way to start building your brand. So, just be careful.

Similar misalignments could be with selling products or offering services that your business hasn't previously promoted. Wildly different new products or market diversification can be handled with sub-branding or launching completely new brands. It all depends on what is appropriate for you as a business and for your existing or prospective customers.

One more thing that could shake the loyalty of your customers is if you decide to team up or align yourself with another organisation that they haven't heard of. Worse still would be to find out sometime down the line that the new "partner" doesn't quite share your philosophical credentials or there are some skeletons in the closet that might not have been divulged.

Such alignments might be with sponsorship (a local football team or awards evening), brand mash-ups (McFlurry) or one off endorsements (offering products or services for an event).

So, what's the best strategy for you when looking at re-positioning diversification, partnering, or sponsoring? Well, like a lot of answers in life "it depends"! It depends on how strong your BRAND is with your current customers and how much they have bought INTO your brand. It will also depend on how you manage your standard communication channels (mail, press, PR, social media etc.) before, during and after you implement some changes. It's always a good idea to keep in touch with your customers, so any change that needs to be announced is also your chance to reach out, discuss the positives of any change to products or services and the benefits to the customer.

APPROPRIATE - STRATEGY QUESTIONS

1. Are you able to gauge your position in your market based on several criteria, i.e. price, quality, speed, comfort, ecological, etc.?

2. How often do you evaluate your price point?

3. Who or what could you team up with/collaborate with/sponsor, with the same or similar passions?

#8 PERCEPTION

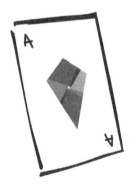

PUNCHING ABOVE YOUR WEIGHT
#8 - A BRAND IS PERCEPTION

As ever, my perception of this chapter is that it should be quite succinct!

You get one chance to make a first impression and there's a lot you can do to create the right impression or perception, way before your customers have even engaged or bought from you. So, let's see what else we can do to get your customers to perceive certain things about your brand.

As the saying goes... PERCEPTION is reality. So whatever your existing or prospective customers think, their experience is going to have an effect on the way they feel about your brand - which they may pass on to a friend.

The perception of your brand is akin to its appropriateness and its reputation. However I do suggest there is a difference.

The appropriateness of your brand is centred around owning a certain position in a market, and you'll continue to make appropriate decisions to ensure you maintain that position. Rationally speaking, this is an objective element that is under your control.

Your reputation, as I outlined previously, is a result or balance of your kept and broken promises. We can therefore say that reputation is an element that you have to manage or steer or monitor after a customer has engaged with you.

In the eyes of your customers the "perception" element of your brand is a double-pronged subjective process. Firstly, their awareness of you is certainly informed by your appropriateness of your marketing and actions. Secondly, the reality of their experience of you and how they share it influences your reputation. I reference the tenth Doctor Who's quote of "*a big ball of wibbly wobbly, timey wimey stuff*" when trying to pin point the perception of your brand at any given point in time. As the Doctor continued, "*It can get away from you!*".

There is also an extra dimension to this element, however. This is where I would urge you to check in on your own perception of your brand from time to time. This element is something that the other building blocks don't touch on as they are very much about objective decision making. Monitoring your own perception or connection with what you're trying to achieve is much overlooked but extremely important. If you don't believe in what you're doing, or trying to achieve, then you can't expect anyone else to. You can somehow convince yourself you enjoy what you're doing, but subconsciously you may be giving off signals that something's amiss, not aligned, out of kilter; and customers and partners alike, may perceive this.

Sit yourself on an imaginary psychiatrist's couch and question your beliefs, philosophies and motivations as to why you're doing what you're doing. Over time, your attitudes, goals, reasons and perceptions of why you started your venture in the first place may have done one of three key things:

1. **Fizzled out**; as it's not as enjoyable as you first imagined or too difficult because you're now having to sort out staff, HR, payroll, and accounts rather than the role you initially envisaged for yourself.

2. **Changed direction**; because of market forces like price of stock, competitors, saturation, culture, ideologies, tech advances, new partners/shareholders etc. This often results in re-positioning in the market.
3. **Become even clearer**; you had a hunch this venture could work and now that belief has been cemented. You may have done things tentatively to begin with but now it's time to commit stronger or more appropriate branding and marketing strategies with better targeting and focus.

There will be others, but in my experience of re-branding companies over the years these are the three "biggies". Owners can get bogged down in so many other business distractions that they just plod on year after year and eventually discover they've lost their confidence and their passion. Their original perception of how wonderful this was going to be has eventually smacked them in the face. However, all is not lost. The above three reasons tend to spark an overhaul of the brand strategy (if you had one in the first place!). Reason one can lead to closure but doesn't always have to. You just need to look for help and advice before it's too late.

Being forced to close because of an imposed lack of customers due to a global pandemic is largely out of anyone's control, so I can't really help with that. Although, as I'm writing this in 2020/21, I'm re-branding and helping companies pivot like mad to get through to the other side. My only non-branding advice is to outsource as much admin as you can as soon as you can. Your payroll, HR, accounting, social media management, website etc. You'll think you're saving money by doing it all yourself, but reason number one to "fizzle out" will most likely arrive at your doorstep much quicker. About 10% of my company's work comes from businesses who have got to this stage, sadly they often get to us too late, and this is another reason I'm sharing my thoughts. An appropriate name, logo or strapline won't save a business alone as there are many reasons why a company will go under. But I'd like to think reading this will save a few.

The triggers for reason two makes up for about 30% of my work. Again, as I'm writing, the eventual final Brexit day looms with huge market forced disruptions for companies who import and export to and from Europe. Many are moving much quicker than the government with "just in case" strategies. It is yet another example of how nimble and flexible businesses have to be to stay afloat. It seems relentless at the moment!

The last reason makes up about 60% of our day to day work, and is another version of "Cornerstone of crap number two": *"Let's start out with not spending too much or doing too much research and see what happens!"* Somehow they've made it thus far and can now afford to concentrate on a proper branding strategy. This usually happens between three to five years, just before 90% of UK businesses fail.

So do check in with yourself every now and then. Talk to other business owners, join director roundtable discussion groups or any business network. Some will say you can learn a great deal from failing. But it's a lot cheaper learning from other people's failures, if they're willing to share!

The emperor's new wardrobe

I imagine you are familiar with the chapter's title "Punching above your weight". The management of perception lies at the heart of this phrase and is usually quite important for start-ups who want to tread tentatively.

In the reputation chapter we touched on a scenario where you had built up a reputation based on a specific skill with friends and family that gave you the impetus to start a business. You may want to start slowly and rely on the existing customers to refer you and you grow steadily and surely. This route clearly isn't always the case. You may start from scratch with no customers, no reputation, just a keen ambition. One common perceptive drawback may instantly present itself, and that's trying to look bigger than you actually are. Although I must stress, I'm only addressing people who feel this could be a problem. For some people, starting small or promoting that they're small may be the correct strategy. For others who are about to compete with some established big hitters, they might want to perceptively "up their game" a little.

Through the marketing of your brand image, you may well want to project a perception that doesn't shout "*Hey I'm just on my own in my front room trying to start a business.*"! You might use images of people smiling, answering phones or shaking hands on your website or leaflets, for instance, rather than the truth of you in your dressing gown with the washing up not yet done from last night. You put on a little "gloss" to begin with. Nothing wrong with that. Along with most business coaches, I would suggest you begin to look, speak and act as you wish to be in a few years, from day one. As I have said previously, you'll get to your goal quicker if you have that mindset. However, what you can't be is completely dishonest.

When I've worked with a new business, I've often asked what other businesses or brands have inspired them or impressed them. Along with that I'd ask what businesses, brands or competitors do they wish to be like at some point in the future. This is useful for a couple of reasons.

Firstly for me, so I can get a rough idea of what they think "good" branding looks like, so I don't completely miss the mark! Although I often have an opportunity to point out where it's not as good as they might think.

More importantly though, it instantly gives the business a visual goal to aim at. Much like pinning an image on a "vision board" as a daily reminder. My job, and therefore yours after reading this book, would be to emulate this visual goal as best you can. Without copyright or trademark infringement or blatant copying of course! When I say, "emulate", I mean identify what you like about it, what you perceive from it and plan out how to re-create similar perceptions. Your customers will perceive all sorts of things from your logo, your name, the quality of your marketing material, the way you dress, the way you answer the phone, your location, your staff... Good and bad. Look and act like the business you wish to be. Success breeds success, look as professional or appropriate as your price point indicates.

Quick fixes to create perceived professionalism

1. Incorporate to a limited company

It's quite easy and relatively inexpensive. Get advice, especially when you have a partner at the moment as you're going to need a shareholders' agreement.

2. Get a registered address

If you don't want to be seen to operate out of a home address, you can either get a P.O. box or use your accountant's office address.

3. Become V.A.T. registered

Not always the case, so get some advice. If you're dealing with domestic customers, then it might not be a good move, because you will instantly be 20% (or whatever it is as you read) dearer than your competition. If you're only dealing with businesses, who will be V.A.T. registered, then it makes no difference.

4. Get some terms and conditions written.

And place them with every quote and invoice.

5. Use professional photography - always helps.

6. Leave a proper business message…

…on your landline and mobile voicemail greeting. Say your name and your business name. Not the auto voice that came with the phone or just inserting your first name when the computer asks you to… awful!!!

7. Get an email address.

That promotes YOUR business name, not Google's.

8. When you refer to yourself…

…use "we" instead of "I" in the marketing copy (although to keep your marketing focused on your customers it's always best to structure the writing around the word "you" as much as you can).

9. Have business meetings…

…in hotel receptions if you wish, or other establishments, or offer to meet the client at their office if you'd rather they didn't meet in your spare bedroom!

10. Follow up within 24 to 48 hours.

With quotes or anything else you said you'd get back on, even if it's just a "nice to have met you".

You may ask what has any of the above got to do with branding? Surely it's just a list of what any business should do, whether they've thought about branding or not. You'd think! However it's actually my list of pet peeves that I find a business doesn't have in place nine times out of ten when we start working with them. It's about perception and therefore it's at least one tenth about branding according to this book! If you want to be perceived as professional, solid, approachable, knowing what you're doing from day one... this list would be a good start. No one has spotted that the emperor isn't wearing the finest of silks in all the land yet, because we're not trying to be something we're not.

Where there's a will there's a way

As a successful example, let's take a start-up in their front room I worked with who had a goal of creating a national master franchise in the wills and LPA market. I was engaged to make them look like a national brand from day one: come up with a name that could be trademarked; the same for the logo; make sure the website reflected the philosophies of the brand; and most importantly make sure it reflects the customer. You don't have to show a fake office or fake receptionist. You can look bigger than you actually are whilst keeping integrity with your actions. Also, by building the experience with your customers by way of efficient, reliable service and simply keeping your promise. Needless to say this particular business, Maplebrook Wills, quickly sold many franchises and had to move into an office suite within a year. Yes, it was hard work on the owner's behalf, and yes it takes investment, but it's not impossible.

Talking of investment, I must stress that whilst you're organising your brand strategy, you will need to consider a marketing budget. This might come as a shock, and I'll be as succinct as possible but....

Marketing creates sales!!

So many businesses I've dealt with think that they will do nothing in terms of marketing to begin with, wait for sales to come in and then start to market themselves from the income of those sales. Even something as simple as creating a website requires a marketing budget to then tell your prospective customers to go and look at it. Creating the site by itself doesn't guarantee anyone will look at it. You may have a name and a logo, but you'll still have to pay someone to print it on some vinyl to then stick onto your van, so you can advertise yourself as you drive around town. Again, there's plenty of books on marketing, so I'll stop there!

The customer is always right?

If you've been in business before, then you'll have a love/hate relationship with this final saying that I'll reference in this chapter. Obviously it's not meant to be taken literally. It just means that, even if they're wrong, it's probably not worth arguing with them. Best to try and understand what the complaint is and offer a suitable response that suits both parties. It's a bit like "I treat people how I expect to be treated". A saying, when taken literally, is actually completely unhelpful. You should treat people how THEY expect to be treated. Because we're all different and wish to be treated differently.

A customer's perception of your business is their reality. So in that world they are right to think and feel what they want. To tap into these thoughts and feelings we need to implement the "customer survey" or versions thereof like a customer feedback form through an email newsletter, even a Doodle poll on Facebook! Feedback and surveys are absolutely crucial to understand the customer's perception of your brand. Feedback often highlights the difference between their perception and yours. I've regularly suggested asking for feedback from customers when re-branding a business, especially when considering re-positioning, diversification or launching new products.

You're about to invest in developing a new product with bigger bells and whistles and perhaps lose a couple of other product lines. The survey then tells you that the product or service you were just about to get rid of is a customer favourite. You may find out that they use a competitor for a certain product because they had no idea that you can offer the same thing. This could be because they don't change habits easily, or that they never received any marketing from you when you launched a new product or service three years ago. Your perception of what's working or benefitting your customer can be very different from theirs. If that perceptive gap becomes a canyon, then your customers will start to drift. I would therefore suggest that consistent communication with your customers through marketing, education and surveys will help fill in the perception void.

Net promoter score

I'll reiterate, just so we're clear: reputation is something you will definitely have. Your customers will have an opinion of you. If strong enough, it will be shared and built; sometimes good, sometimes bad and you'll know about it either way. Below these strong reactions are slight perceptions of you that might not be of too much concern to them, but could be useful to you. As described above, your customer assumes you don't have a certain product, even if you do, and buys it elsewhere but isn't too bothered. Luckily there is a system that can measure exactly how fussed all your customers collectively are. This can then tell you how likely your customers are to recommend you to their contacts. That system is called the "net promoter score". It is often used by marketeers hand-in-hand with customer surveys.

I won't go into the ins and outs as that's for a marketing book to explain. However I'll do the short version. It's as simple as surveying your customers and asking them to give you a score out of 10 as to the likelihood of them recommending you to their friends and colleagues, i.e. "promote" you. You then take away the cumulative 0-6 scores (detractors) away from your 9-10 scores (promoters) and you get the 'Net' score. Customers who score you at 7 or 8 are called passives. If you thought scoring 7 or 8 was good, then think again, you've got to be better than that! You then work out this as a percentage of the overall numbers who took part in the survey.

Here's the scary news. Or if you've read certain parts of the book already, it comes as no shock that the average score for a UK company hovers around 30%. Therefore most businesses in the UK have a majority of customers who are very unlikely to promote them in a positive light. They could still promote them because of low ticket reasons like cheapness, distance, convenience, habitualness. With the right branding strategy you'll want your customers to be positively frothing at the mouth when they tell their friends about you. You don't really want them saying:

"Yeah, they're alright".

These types of customers are often termed as "raving fans" and I'm certain there are a few books about that!

The highest NPS company I've worked with is 97%, and many are from 60% upwards, which is good. Always room for improvement though.

Perceived competition

Lastly (I think), let's hark back to the saying at the start of the chapter "perception is reality". You may (or indeed should) have an idea who your "direct" competitors are. The companies who sell the same product or service as you do, to the same target audiences. Add to this: possibly in the same geographic location and even at a very similar price. Then there is another level of "perceived" competitors. You'll know that they are not directly competing with you, but prospective customers might not, and that's the difference.

Take a quick "Google search" of photographers in your geographical location, for instance, and see what turns up. If they are all photographers and they all take photographs, they must perceivably be in competition with each other? Well, of course, that won't necessarily be the case. A wedding photographer is not in direct competition with a product photographer. A studio-only based family portrait photographer is not in direct competition with a location events photographer, and so on. But a prospective customer won't know that initially. Also, when finding businesses through search engines, the companies who arrive in the top ten list on page one might only be there because of how good they are at search engine optimisation (S.E.O.) rather than how good they are at photography. What I'm trying to illustrate here is that your prospective audience may combine your perceived competitors in with your direct competitors. The end result of this being that, in their eyes, you're now competing with companies who you don't really think you compete with. You may even lose out to them. This possible confused perception is why the individual building blocks like Difference and Appropriateness are so important. Finding that focused or niche gap in the market and really owning it so there can be no confusion between you and your perceived competitors will certainly help create a stronger brand.

Do what you say you're going to do

As a business owner, you will have so many things to control to build your brand. The 99 or so things you're getting right on a daily basis will make you feel you're doing a great job.

However your customer only needs one thing to go wrong and their whole perception of your brand, and their emotional connection with you, may change. So just be aware that bad word of mouth travels 11 times quicker than good word of mouth. So what can you do to keep your customers' perception of you as intact as possible? Well, I believe there are two levels at which we all operate; the things we say and things we do. Our promises, and our actions. Stick to your principles and values, and don't try to be something you're not.

PERCEPTION - STRATEGY QUESTIONS

1. When was the last time you surveyed your customers? And was it done via an external agency?If you conduct your own surveys you may not get to the truth because your customer won't want to offend you directly.

2. What "graphical packaging" (logo, colours, photos) or "marketing collateral" (business cards, leaflets, adverts) enables you to look like your price point?

3. What do you have in place to react quickly to customer complaints?

#9 CONSISTENT

IT'S ONLY A CUP OF COFFEE

#9 - A BRAND IS CONSISTENT

This element of BRANDING is one of those seemingly easy concepts that really upsets me. I'm repeatedly surprised when I see inconsistency within businesses as I know it's going to lose the companies money. I'll make that clearer by saying: a business will be missing opportunities that they didn't know they could have had and will therefore have lost money.

Consistent service

Firstly we'd better establish what is meant by an inconsistency. The easiest example I think we can all relate to would be inconsistent customer service. Let's say we go to our favourite restaurant. This time we've also invited some friends and the service is not as good as you've experienced in the past. It was good the last time you dined there and today it's bad, and boom! We have an inconsistency. Hopefully that's an obvious and clear example, but let's break that down a bit into what else has actually happened and how it could impact on the brand.

The damage of this inconsistency is dependent on how the experience was encountered. The key elements were:

- It's our favourite restaurant.
- The service has always been good.
- We've invited our friends - who we know, like and trust. They could be work colleagues, they could be our clients.

If it's a favourite restaurant, it may be that we've been there several times; and prior to that it may have been recommended to us or we've noticed it a few times through marketing or reviews; and at some point we decided to give it a go.

So crucially, in this scenario, the relationship between the customer and brand has been built over time. It's strong, it's confident, it's trusted. Then, out of nowhere the implied promise or contract of a "good service" has been broken. Not only have I been let down, I've also been embarrassed in front of my friends or clients. One's pride has been hurt so inevitably, as the saying goes, comes the fall! The stronger the initial bond, may suggest the longer and harder the fall.

We tend not to keep this sort of experience to ourselves. As humans we want to tell someone else about our misfortune, especially when the service has been bad. Not only that, in this scenario four or five people are going to spread that bad word. Oh, and it gets worse - when we hit the inter web and compose impassioned and inflammatory reviews for the whole world to see. There's another psychological layer which comes into play that most of us may not be aware of, and that's where we have subconsciously let ourselves down. Consciously, we can quickly blame the restaurant for not providing the level of service we expected, but "deep down" we are also blaming ourselves for placing that level of expectation on the restaurant in the first place. Weirdly, we feel it's partly our fault!

I have often said to my son, *"Lower your expectations of everything and everyone and you'll never be disappointed"*. I've also been told that's a pessimistic way to look at the world and I should have more faith! Everyone's allowed to look at the world however they want, so I'm not suggesting you should take my advice on that view! It depends on your nature of course.

Takeaway customers

The reason I pick the restaurant scenario is because I have worked a great deal in the hospitality sector. I love the immediacy of feedback with the customer and the task that myself and the owner have to create, that most elusive of unicorns, "customer loyalty". All of this constantly hangs in the balance for the very reason of the above scenario. Thanks to a combination of Adam Smith and Napoleon, the UK has been referred to as "a nation of shopkeepers" whilst simultaneously and paradoxically being acknowledged by most consumers for awful levels of service.

I outlined at the start of this chapter that inconsistency will lose you money. When I get in front of the employees of a coffee shop, this is where the missed opportunities really highlight themselves. Let me take an even smaller scenario than the restaurant. Picture a customer and their friend walk up to the counter. Instead of a "Hello", they just get an upwards nod and a lukewarm cup of coffee. They decide not to visit again. I would then ask the staff, *"What's the lost opportunity?"*.

Sadly, most would say *"Well, they paid for the coffee, so nothing has been lost"*. Thankfully some staff would grasp the idea that if those customers don't visit again then there are *"A few cups of coffee that won't be bought"*.

A FEW!!!

This new employee didn't realise in this coffee shop scenario, that the customer always bought their lunchtime sandwich, crisps and orange juice at least three times a week. They were popping in at a different time with a friend they had just bumped into. The shortfall of takings is now £10.00 a week, or at the very least £500 for the year, and that's just lunch. That's not counting the other possible weekend coffees and muffins and lunches with family and friends. Then there is the biggest loss of income - when the customer stops recommending the cafe and their friend now starts spreading bad word of mouth. The cafe has potentially lost thousands of pounds and the staff think it's just a couple of cups of coffee. You can also therefore imagine what the ongoing missed opportunities or cash that the previous restaurant scenario had lost out on.

Reading this, you may well have heard of actual "service level agreements" within certain businesses, those usually offering a retained service. This is where, as a customer, you can exactly set your expectations of the brand. This is because it's been written down and you now have a set of guidelines, at a chosen level of cost to you, where you have recourse to address a complaint if you have been let down. Hopefully the brand will take control and be proactive about ensuring delivery of the agreed level of service you were expecting. In a restaurant or even a cafe you can of course refuse to pay or, if the owner has any common sense, they can offer the goods for free. Losing £5 or £30 is nothing compared to the future loss of £000s! As in the "Reputation" chapter, you need systems and procedures in place when things go wrong. For me however, the absolute priority is the training of staff and to get their buy-in to your brand. If they're not happy in their job, find out why before they start losing you money.

These scenarios are demonstrating the possible tragic and sad end of the customer journey due to a "little inconsistency" in service on just one day. The bigger minefield of consistency is actually at the start of building the brand.

A consistent message

You may have heard or read the adage that "It takes around seven marketing touches to get a prospective customer to even acknowledge you exist, let alone buy from you." You need a loyal customer to actually buy INTO you, but let's not get ahead of ourselves.

This book won't advise on a marketing strategy per se, but let's take a few obvious ways we can reach out to prospective customers. A leaflet, a social media post, a bus advert, an email, a website, a shop front and a business card let's say. You might even choose to just carry out seven touches of one method. I would suggest doing a few because you can then gauge which method is working best for you, when comparing the conversion rates.

The marketing materials themselves should have consistent elements, no matter if they are created for different platforms, sizes and uses.

If we look back at the list of elements that should be "original" or at least "different", we can separate them into two groups. Elements that your customer will engage with at a glance or sub-consciously:

- Logo
- Company name
- Company strapline
- Colour scheme
- Typefaces
- Photography
- Illustrations/cartoons

and elements that customers have to consciously engage with:

- Headline/sub heading

- Body copy
- Calls to action: phone, email, website

As we have been observed, your customer will need to see the above combination of elements around seven times to even acknowledge your existence. Some businesses seem to think it's a good idea to be different and fresh each time they do some marketing... Well it's not! Especially in the early days of trying to brand new customers. You can, of course, have different marketing campaigns, selling different products; but the basic design, size of heading, where the logo is, colouring etc. needs to be very familiar each and every time.

Are you talking to me?

Even decades after big brands have launched, they know that being consistent is key to keeping their brand awareness firmly at the forefront of the minds of their customers. Sainsbury's are still using orange, Compare the Market still use a meerkat, Nike still ask you to "Just Do It".

The basics of a logo, typeface, colour etc. are not the only elements to keep consistent when you market or present your business. There are two other crucial elements to keep consistent in a business, and they are

your "messaging" and your "tone of voice" or personality. We established in the "passion" and "promise" chapters that you should stand for something, have a value system and keep your promises. So it should stand to reason that you must be consistent in the delivery of those elements as well.

We have previously established that a brand will want to convey certain messages to attract the right audience. Sometimes, in quite a generic market with huge competition, it will be difficult to have differentiating messages like speed, price, heritage, diversity and so on. But whatever they are, stick to them! Continually and consistently concentrate on your story when communicating any message.

An element that may differentiate you from your competitor is your business's personality or "tone of voice". If you want to be known for being "cheerful and playful" or "Informative and friendly" then that personality needs to be consistent across all interactions. I've read a business website or brochure that is full of industry jargon and quite awful platitudes of corporate nonsense like "delivering customer solutions". I then phone them up and find those words don't represent them at all.

From the writing style on your website and brochures, to the answer machine message and the way your staff talk to your customers, it all needs to feel as if it comes from the same imaginary person. I'd always recommend working with a professional copywriter for all your marketing communications as they understand this crucial aspect of connecting with your customers. A copywriter will also create, what their industry call, "buyer persona" profiles for your customers who have different behavioural styles, motivations and needs. You'll know exactly how to communicate with them on their terms to get the best engagement combined with your established brand personality.

It might sound calculated but it's just common sense. Just take notice of how you might act when being introduced to someone new, for example. Whether socially or in a business environment, you are most likely to introduce yourself or start a conversation in much the same way you have always done. If you're a strong confident extrovert you'll probably stretch out your hand first, begin a firm handshake (or elbow?), state your name in a way that you've always said. It's who you are and it always will be, with slight degrees of variation. Although I expect there will be a more noticeable change in your behaviour if you were introduced to the Queen or a similar VIP.

The point being is, the next time you meet that person they will expect you to have the same manners, behaviours, way with words, facial tics and all!! So I'm merely suggesting you recognise that familiarity we have at a human level and replicate it through all your communications with your customers to keep them at ease and comfortable with your brand.

Consistency is key. Resist the temptation to change or fiddle, just because you're a bit fed up that your last three adverts looked the same. You've still got another four more to go because most of your prospective customers haven't noticed any of them yet. If you're not consistent, nothing has been built, so please hang in there!

CONSISTENT - STRATEGY QUESTIONS

1. What are your core messages and how do you communicate them to your audience? If a core message is "speed" for instance, then you may say that on your website. But how quickly do you answer a phone or get back with an enquiry?

2. How do the words on your website compare to the language on the phone / in person / via your staff?

3. Compare your business card / website / shop front / marketing collateral - are they all IDENTICAL? Do a quick audit, check colours, typefaces, grammar... are circles circular or are they oval sometimes?

#10 VALUE

MAKE SURE IT'S WORTH IT

#10 - A BRAND IS VALUE

We're here. Number ten out of ten. A book that has literally taken 25 years to conceive, and we're tantalizingly close to having blurted all my thoughts out!

First of all, I'd better identify what types of "values" we're going to discuss in this chapter. I've certainly mentioned the word throughout the book and possibly said I'd explain further in this chapter. So, I'd better!

There are a few definitions of the word "value" but I'm going to concern us with the following two interpretations.

Economic value
and
Moral value

These two can then be broken down a little further, for the purposes of identifying the part they play in brand building.

Economic value

1. The actual cost/price of your services or products.
2. The worth your customers then assign to your services or products.

3. The monetary worth of your business and its associated brand assets if it was for sale.

Moral value

1. The values you live by and believe in.
2. The values that your employees have.
3. The value you, your business and your staff provide to your customer that are not monetarily based e.g. advice, comfort, experience, knowledge and so on.

VALUE - PART ONE

ECONOMIC VALUE

Forgive me if you've heard this before, but I'd like to share something that opened my eyes from a Sandler Training sales course many years ago. The trainer exclaimed:

"COST is never the issue when your prospect exclaims your service or product is too much."

The "issue" is: the value they've assign to the cost of your service or product simply doesn't match up. Most people sum up this assessment with:

"It's just not worth it." (there's a strapline in there, I'm sure!!!)

The trainer then demonstrated exactly how this can be explained. This bit is so clever, yet so simple.

If I tried to sell you a brand new, off-the-shelf, ordinary Mars Bar for £500 would you buy it?

The answer would be an emphatic *"NO!"*. O.K. let's try something else.

If I tried to sell you a brand new BMW Series 8 coupe for £500 would you buy it?

159

Even if you didn't need one, you'll say yes, and then sell it on perhaps!

The point here is quite clear. The cost is exactly the same in each offering, it hasn't changed. What has changed is the value assigned to the purchase by the buyer. In this scenario a Mars Bar is not worth £500 and a brand new car clearly is. The chapter on perception is important because it explains other elements which are in play here as well. The prospective purchaser will quickly dismiss the cost of the Mars bar as being ridiculous. They may equally think the cost of the car is ridiculous, but it won't be dismissed out of hand. The next likely thought may be one of suspicion and a question of *"What's the catch?"*.

Admittedly this is an extreme example to make the point, but a clear one: in any transaction "cost" is never the issue. It really isn't. Therefore nothing is "too expensive" and nothing is "too cheap". Maybe, like you, I've been asked in the past *"Are you expensive?"* or I've offered a price in the past and a response has been *"Sounds a bit cheap!"*. At the extremes of commerce, you can certainly be the most expensive or the absolute cheapest, but market forces will quickly tell you that your service or product is "too" one or the other. You'll either stop trading because you never sell anything, or you'll go bust because your outgoings are more than your incomings. This is why we do some research, find out what things cost to manufacture or what the overheads are to provide a service; take a look at what cost the competitors are selling at; and pick a "reasonable" price to sell at that suits us.

What are you worth?

When I have been asked *"Are you expensive?"* I've learned to:

a) Bite my tongue, and
b) Say in my head, and sometimes out loud:

"No, I offer great value for money."

My products or services are only perceptively too expensive or too cheap based on the buyer's concept of value, not mine. It could also be based on their upbringing, what they earn, how much disposable income they have, their belief systems and so on.

I have zero interest in cars, for instance. So to spend over £100,000 on one (let alone £20,000) seems mind-bogglingly ridiculous to me. However, that's irrelevant to a millionaire who has that sort of change lost in the back of their sofa and will buy one as a present to say sorry on Valentine's Day. It's all relative.

Another great lesson given to me was to learn or appreciate my own worth or self-value, and to then be comfortable to put a price on that. I'm not suggesting we have to cost ourselves and reduce everyone down to a price tag! Conventionally for my trade, I charge by the hour for my services; so I have to understand what value I bring to my clients and put a price on that. This took me quite some time and I did struggle with why I didn't value myself in the early days. But maybe that's for another more confessional book!!

The easy answer for not being able to value my worth is that, early on I clearly didn't have the experience in my field compared to what I have to offer 25 years later, so I probably charged accordingly. You may have heard of Malcolm Gladwell's popularisation of the 10,000 hours concept. When practicing a skill or discipline for that magical number of hours, you are likely to become an "expert" or "professional" or even a "world-class master of that skill". This is easily relatable to something like a musician, which can be perfectly demonstrated when you watch and hear someone playing. Can they play violin really well? Yes they can! They got that good by putting in the hours. Could I charge for advice on branding, designing a logo and creating a strapline on the first day of opening my business? Well of course I could. I had a degree in graphic design and nine years working as a graphic designer with four years of that as a creative director. The big question was, how much? Unlike the Mars Bar/BMW anecdote, the answer lies in between much tighter boundaries, but boundaries nevertheless. You'll no doubt test out and trial pricing until you find what works, as well as what you are comfortable with.

Obviously there's a difference between practising a violin and developing brands for businesses, but I'd considered that I clocked up my 10,000 hours of branding work by about year five in my own business, let alone the nine years previous. Ten hours a day (minimum), 22 days a month (on average) multiplied by 11 months (four weeks holiday, that's a joke!) multiplied by five years. Luckily around this point I did some work with a business coach called Jill Green, who I'm very grateful to for having the "value" discussion with me. She taught me to value myself, look at what I was providing and what value that gave to my clients. We also discussed what further value I could add, and in doing so could I possibly change my pricing accordingly. Suffice to say the business model did change quite a bit after that!

Start as you mean to go on

As I've pointed out, we all value things differently. It's all relative. Unlike working out margins and balancing profit and loss accounts, there is no definitive formula to work out how you value what you do. One reason why I'm writing a chapter on value at all, is to highlight that it would be useful to learn to value yourself earlier than I did. Once you've "evaluated" how much value you provide your customers and what cost you feel is suitable to set against it, comes the biggest challenge - sticking to it!

The ultimate test as to whether you have truly costed the value you provide correctly is whether people buy your offer at the set price. If your customers start to negotiate, drive you down or go elsewhere, have you got the pricing wrong? Possibly, but another answer could be that you simply haven't clearly communicated the level of value they will get. It may not have been explained through your marketing or the branding is too much like a competitor or isn't appropriate, so the perception is that your offer will be of similar price. Hence why the previous chapters were written to lead us to this point.

Once you are truly happy with your offer, its inherent value and its price point, the worst thing you can do is to cave as soon as someone asks you to do it cheaper just to make a sale. The instant you agree to do it for less than advertised or match a competitor's price you instantly devalue yourself, your service or product.

Of course we have all done it and it can backfire in another way. You may be familiar with a scenario where you have wobbled at a price and before you know it, the trader has knocked off 10, 20 or 50%. My instant reaction when this happened to me wasn't one of:

"I've got myself a great deal.", it was more of:

"Wow they were going to rip me off for another £200!"

That instant crash in price did the seller no favours at all. They weren't devaluing themselves, they were simply trying to get as much money out of me as possible, knowing all the time how low they could go.

You'll experience this with the likes of some annual renewals like phones or insurance. You ring up, say you think the new price is a bit steep and often they'll very quickly offer you a better price. This will be because the company has calculated that a much bigger percentage of customers won't even see the increase. It's planned that the smaller percentage of lower prices will be paid for by the vast unseen increases. They'll be happy to take the odd phone call from "outraged of Milton Keynes". Another ruse would be the car showroom's classic line of, *"I'll just have a word with my boss to see what I can do"*.

More or less

There is of course a tradition of "negotiating" or "haggling" that is enjoyed by some people, so I'm not telling you to never change the price. I'm probably saying be aware of what message you're putting out and what precedents you could be setting by instantly devaluing yourself or your goods. There certainly may be some situations where supposedly rigid price structures may have to be flexible. The trick or strategy would be to outline the parameters very clearly when asked to do something for less than previously advertised. Here are a few examples:

Just this once

Make it clear this is a one-off instance and you wouldn't ordinarily do it.

If there is an invoice involved, write on it that it's a special discount. There'll be no quibble the next time they ask you to do it again or they say *"But you did it for such a price last time"*. You'll have the evidence!

As a favour

This is more in the realms of barter, and as a form of business negotiation, ask for something in return; now or sometime in the future. My closest customers know I'll do almost anything for a bottle of Honey Jack!

• • •

Do less

For a service industry, such as mine, I put in a quote to produce some work and customers have said *"Is there any room for manoeuvre?"*. I'll have to quote Sandler Training again here:

"Yes of course, how much MORE would you like to pay?"

Try it with a straight face and see what happens! Back in the real world, the customer clearly means they want a cheaper price. You can still say *"Yes, of course"*, then instead, you could add:

1. I'll just work the hours your budget gives me (rather than how long I know I need to do the job, hence why I quoted what I quoted in the first place!).
2. Instead of six options we'll do four.
3. Instead of turning the work round in three days, we'll stretch it over two weeks.
4. Instead of paying us all of the cost on completion, I'll offer you to spread it over three separate payments to help your cashflow.

Essentially, try to achieve a "win-win" outcome.

In the first three cases, if the price has now changed then other parameters will have to change. In case "d" you haven't budged on price, but you have given the customer a changed parameter in payment to help them.

If you're familiar with what is sometimes known as the "Sales triangle (of death)" or the "Good, fast & cheap" principle, then you'll know that you have three parameters to play with in any transaction of goods and services: quality, time and price. The two guiding principles to remember are:

1. You can't have all three working in the customer's

favour - you'll get trampled on and eventually go out of business.

2. The customer can prioritise two parameters but will have to accept the consequence of the third.

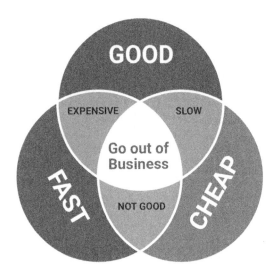

For example, if your customer wants your service or product to be:

- Quick and of high quality (fast and good) it will be expensive.
- Inexpensive and of high quality (cheap and good) it will take longer.
- Quick and inexpensive (fast and cheap) it will be of low quality.

If you keep this principle in mind, you won't reduce your value, you'll be negotiating a way to keep it intact.

• • •

Winter of discounted tents

The more acceptable ways of seemingly devaluing your offer are of course the "January sales" the "BOGOF" (buy one get one free) or variations thereof like "2 for 1" or "cheaper item free", "meal deals" etc. There could be very reasonable economical and commercial reasons for these options. End of season fashion items, getting rid of old stock before the new stuff, close to sale-by date food items. In some cases you might be employing a "loss leader" technique to attract customers to buy something else or get them interested in a product that will increase in price at a later date once they're "hooked". I know...evil!! I'm not condoning, I'm merely highlighting!

Price match

Marketeers will say this is a very effective way of not losing customers along with "free shipping", and I'm not going to argue. I'm trying to offer you the building blocks to create loyal customers, not just keep customers. You can always be cheaper or the exact same price as your competition if push comes to shove. What intrigues me is how these campaigns often spend their marketing budgets on actually giving their competitors some exposure.

Vouchers and coupons

Here you'll be trying to attract new customers by offering the product or service for less than usual. To me this form of discounting moves into the realms of a marketing strategy, which should have an assigned marketing budget. I therefore wholeheartedly recommend such a strategy!

———

Customer loyalty

A. Familiar bits of cardboard to entice you to collect nine coffee stamps to get your tenth latte on the house. This particular concept tries to create loyalty from the first moment you walk into a shop, rather than rewarding a customer for their loyalty after a long period of time.

B. Then there's the complete opposite like George Clooney's character in *Up In The Air* receiving his elite membership credit card to instantly upgrade any flight after clocking up 10 million air miles. This actually did happen to US car salesman Thomas Stuker which took him 29 years to get his reward. The result of this becomes a big PR campaign, so back in the realms of marketing.

C. Collecting points that turn into pounds on a Sainsbury's Nectar card or a Tesco Clubcard which you can set against your shopping whenever you wish.

D. Cashback cards like Utility Warehouse where you can receive discounts from high street shops if you use their card rather than a credit or debit card. The savings you make then come off your utility bill.

Friends go free

You may be a gym member and see a scheme that encourages you to refer a friend to collect a free massage. I would again place this tactic firmly in the marketing strategy corner. This just needs to be tracked to see if it's working. Remember, if no one gets recommended, you won't be giving away free stuff, so ultimately you might not be devaluing anything.

I think that's enough examples for you to get the point. They are all completely acceptable ways of encouraging customers to spend their money with you rather than a competitor and keep coming back, sometimes under the pretence of "loyalty". I also think most of you reading this will understand that there's no such thing as a free lunch, and we're pretty sure these companies aren't really giving things away for free. They'll be making up the difference somewhere else. Whether you feel the need, or strategically plan to offer a discount here and there, all I advise is that you set clear parameters of how long the discount will last. Show expiry dates, make sure the customer knows it's for a limited time. Unlike a certain sofa company, you don't want a reputation for constantly discounting. You'll find it very hard to convince your customers of your worth when, for a short period of time, you don't actually discount yourself.

Taking price off the table

I'm guessing you're now screaming at this page…

"O.K. you've told us not to cut our prices, so how do we create value and stop people asking us to do it cheaper?"

Good scream!

There are a few basics that we have actually gone through in this book already, so I'll put those elements into focus and start with the absolute tangible. If you know about the laws of supply and demand you'll know that something in short supply with a high demand creates high value and vice versa. In essence:

"Scarcity creates value."

That's why I've talked about being original or at least being different. Having an original name, different message, original approach, different benefit and so on. If you've at least chipped away at these tangible, identifiable tasks and your competitors haven't, then you have begun to create scarcity. I know that sounds simplistic, but the simplicity of this basic principle of supply and demand can't be ignored.

"In the land of the blind, the one-eyed will rule."

In a 99% male dominated land of average plumbers, mostly named with three forgettable letters, the all women plumbing franchise "Stopcocks" (brilliant name!!) is going to instantly be of more value, especially to a female audience. There may be one tangible element in your business you can make scarce like the aforementioned "Stopcocks" model, or you may have to look at several items to create scarcity. But it can be done.

Getting your individual products or services to become valuable will in turn increase the overall value of your business, which is often called (warning jargon ahead) BRAND EQUITY.

Where most businesses are shouting about WHAT they do and they've all got blue logos (cos that's what they think their market should look like!), they become part of an oversupply of averageness... if they're lucky. If you stand out, you concentrate on the WHY and you consistently deliver on your promises, then you can become a scarce commodity. You and I inherently know this to be true, I'm just urging you to consider it after reading this book.

I've noticed I keep distinguishing between a product or service based industry because in commerce this is what we've been taught. We've also been taught other models like business to business (B2B) or business to consumer (B2C), and I suspect many more. All models aside, and whether you think you're a product based company, in the end it will be your levels of service that will ultimately give you the opportunity to increase the value you provide to your customer. I'm sure you've encountered or transacted with hundreds of companies and I've certainly worked with hundreds. It's rare when you are bowled over by truly excellent levels of service, but so easy to implement. You don't have to do a lot to stand out.

"A product based business increases its value by increasing its level of service, not its products."

Let me elaborate.

You may well think you're a product based business because you sell mattresses or reams of A4 copier paper or fruit and veg. However, I'm willing to bet that plenty of businesses have competitors that sell exactly the same products. Therefore a prospective customer can, in this instance, literally compare apples to apples. Let's accept that the apple or mattress or paper is in good condition, the right colour, the required size and shape. In my experience, and the reason I actually picked these three products, is that the businesses in question could be a re-seller and all of them are using the same wholesaler. So they literally are the exact same products. I've already tried my hardest to suggest you don't instantly leap to compete on price, so that leaves levels of service: Politeness, speed, quality of delivery (if using shipping), accommodation of special requests, reactions and policies for returns and refunds etc. The prospective customer is then left with a clear choice. They can either buy a product with an average service or, for the same price, a great service. Remember the cost hasn't changed, the appreciation of the associated value has.

Just like Domino's isn't in the pizza business, it's firmly in the delivery game. Product based or not, it will be advantageous to think you're in a service industry first and foremost.

Big brands, big money

Yes, I know, you're probably also screaming…

"Hang on a minute, how come the big brands like Apple and Nike, actually charge a hell of a lot MORE than their competitors - sometimes their products are the same (or worse even)?"

Well my good friends, that certainly can be the eventual outcome. Let's not run before we can walk. A customer will buy FROM you if you're cheap enough and they'll accept the bad product quality and service for a low price, but I want your customers to buy INTO you. I want them to buy into the value of what's behind your brand, the price your offer is "almost" taken off the table and can increase to accommodate the associated costs of the extra levels of value. The branding strategies of Apple and Nike were no different at the start of their journey from what's in this book. Consistent, differentiating messaging to the target audience. Their later marketing strategies show associations with great thought leaders (in the case of Apple) or great athletes (Nike) and this association becomes part of the intrinsic value of the brand. The customer will transfer their newly acquired emotional attachment and convert it into perceived extra value. They will be happy to pay for this.

A brief warning from history

You could say that such strategies are manipulative and evil - Naomi Klein certainly did in her book *No Logo*. Back in 1999 she quite rightly brought to light the globalisation tactics by big brands such as these. To my mind it's not that using Michael Jordan in the marketing to get you to buy the latest "Air" is so horrible; it's the exploitative actions to produce the "Air" that's the obvious problem.

The big brands out there do tend to get too greedy, profit driven and then ultimately, it would seem, exist for their shareholders more than their customers. They charge well over the odds and production costs are the lowest possible because of practically slave labour. I think, 20 years after No Logo, and numerous other exposés, we're unfortunately familiar with stories of suicide nets on factories in China; and Bangladesh sweatshop factory collapses. So, let's learn from that.

I hope I'm making it clear that I'm trying to help start-ups and small businesses, not global giants here. I'll reiterate what I said at the end of the "perception" chapter. There are two levels at which we all operate; the things we say and things we do: our promises, and our actions. Stick to your principles and values (we'll come onto the other meaning of value soon), and don't be something you're not.

"What's good for the pocket could be bad for the soul.".

Trademarking

Back in the "perception" chapter I wrote a list of things you can do to increase your credibility or perception of professionalism and, indeed, intrinsic value. I left one out to keep for this chapter and I have promised throughout that I would eventually expand further.

Not to be confused with "copyrighting"; protection of intellectual property which itself gets confused with "copywriting", re-arranging words to make things sell better! Copyright literally boils down to "only the owner of the idea (or other authorised parties) have the right to reproduce (copy) their idea". A trademark is a "tangible 'mark' (drawing, motif, image) that represents, symbolises or is associated with their trade". To add a level of confusion there are two symbols you may be familiar with:

TM and ®

Both symbols are often seen next to a logo but only ® gives you protection. The TM symbol is merely saying to the onlooker *"Hey, you see that logo I'm next to? That's what we use to represent our business."*, i.e. that's the "mark" of our "trade". And that's all it's doing. It serves no protection. It's a bit like an empty pretend alarm box on the side of your building. It gives the illusion that you have security and it may deter a burglar. In this analogy, it may stop a competitor copying it, but if they know the differences between TM and ®, then it won't.

A "TM" is a trademark symbol and a ® is a registered trademark symbol. Sprinkled through the book, I've mentioned granting a trademark for a logo or strapline or a name and we've now reached the explanation. Yet another way to increase the value of your brand is to protect the elements that can be shielded from competitors trading off the goodwill and trust that you build over time with your customers.

As I've demonstrated in the "different" chapter, people will do their best to copy you, if you are successful. They will try to entice your customers away from you by pretending to be you through very similar branding. You may well say that you don't plan to be so successful and that would never happen. Alas, I've seen it when dealing with small independent businesses in Bristol that I've worked for. Almost an endorsement of how good our work is, where we could have taken the stance that imitation is the sincerest form of flattery. Not in business!

By protecting the tangible assets of your brand (name, logo, strapline) through trademarking, you are in a much stronger position to stop competitors trying to copy you by the formal legal instruction of "cease and desist".

This is a double protection as well:

First protection:

You stop a competitor taking your customers or at least stopping the confusion of your customer's friends trying to seek you out for the first time and accidentally going to the competitor.

Second protection:

If it's the case that the competitor is providing an inferior product or service, you then stop their bad reputation rubbing off on to yours.

There are a few reasons that a trademark will then tangibly increase the value of your business:

1. We've mentioned the perceived increase in professionalism.
2. The ability to shut down copycats keeps you scarce.
3. If you intend to sell, the buyer will be glad you're already protected which will increase the value of the sale.
4. Similarly if you want to create a franchise, the value of a licence will have increased in value.

The process

So, how do you get that "R" in a circle next to your logo? Well, it's really quite a simple process. It takes between three to eight months depending on objections. If you get a solicitor to do it, it's going to cost about £500 and it will last for ten years. Like every industry please be aware of misinformation or doing it yourself for less. Especially if a website says they can "copyright" your logo for £37. Hopefully you now know, someone clearly doesn't know what they're talking about. I've just found such a website whilst writing this bit!

The reason I bang on about originality or being as different as possible is for the process of scarcity and for trademarking. The more unique (I know you can't say that, but I just have!) your brand assets are, the higher chance of getting a registered trademark. You may not know this but there are also 45 separate "classes" in which you can have your trademark protected. This is why you really need a solicitor to make sure they assign your trademark to the right class and outline the exact descriptive parameters of what you are clearly protecting within that class. Having a trademark class system also allows for some non-original thought, which I will be totally against, but I'll explain.

You may have heard of a brand called Polo or Oasis, but you might not be thinking of the one I'm thinking of. Here's a clear example of how the trademark classes work. Polo mints can exist in one class at the same time as Polo cars and Polo shirts. Oasis the band can exist in another class to the Oasis clothes store or Oasis the soft drink. A brand will be perfectly within its right to object at a registration for a trademark in the same name if they can prove that their customers will get confused. In the above cases, Volkswagen would have to prove that a customer could walk into their car showroom and wonder why they couldn't buy a packet of mints. Or a customer would go to a ticket tout and be surprised when they didn't receive a bottle of squash. Clearly this can't be proved and we are all happy for these exact same names to exist and we are not confused at all. The above examples will have their trademarks registered in different classes, so this provides a little room for similarity that is proven not to impact. So, it's possible, but as a start-up or SME do you really want to have the hassle or take the risk? It definitely all hots up when you try to register the same name in the same class.

In conclusion don't think about it, don't work hard for two or three years, have a great looking brand, to then have someone else copy all your hard work and start taking your customers or trample on your reputation.

VALUE - PART TWO

MORAL VALUE

No doubt there are endless books and online articles about brand values, so I'm not going to recite or try to put a different spin on them. I would hopefully have already outlined on many occasions in this book the concept of tapping into your personal moral values as a foundation for your business. Be it in the "passion" or "promise" chapter, or further on in the separate strapline chapter, I've asked…

"What do you stand for?"

Having asked this of many directors I know it's difficult. It's not something most parents discuss with their children. It's not something we discuss in early education. I don't ever recall sharing my deep seated values with my mates in a pub either. You might not have ever given this topic a first or second thought. Our inherent values or moral compass tend to evolve overtime and can present themselves without us really knowing how they got there or how to label them. They will however bubble up to the surface, possibly when you least expect it. A casual conversation about capital punishment or organ donation perhaps? You will have a view. You may not know when that view or opinion was established or how it formed. You can't really be sure if it's totally yours or something inherited. In your world there will be things that are right and wrong, behaviours that are justified or not. As you grow up, initially possibly to your surprise, other people will have different perspectives on your version of right and wrong and over a pint you may be challenged. This may strengthen, mould or completely change your previously held beliefs. That's fine. As human beings we are allowed to learn and grow. We're not who we were yesterday and certainly not who we were ten years ago, despite the current cancel culture. I'm not going to pretend to be an expert on the interactions of cultural and societal morals and ethics, and how they interact or impact on an individual's value system. As with other topics in here, that's for another more qualified author, but I recommend you do a deep dive someday!

My task here is to help you recognise that it's important to:

- Realise that as a business owner you have a set of values, and
- To really think about using these values to create the foundation of your brand and then to use them to build on it and aid decision-making!

When I've asked a business owner *"What do you stand for?"* there's often been quite a period of silence, reflection, grunts and groans. Finally they say a few things that they clearly feel they should say. Over many years of asking, here's the top ten:

1. Service
2. Excellence
3. Honesty
4. Integrity
5. Trustworthiness
6. Knowledge
7. Quality

8. Competitiveness
9. Passion
10. Innovation

You may well say what a great list. I, however, will say that at least seven of them are prerequisites for running a business in the first place. Having "service" at the top kind of validates my opinion that every business is in the business of service. The rest… c'mon, really?

I know I'm being harsh and I had clearly put them on the spot. So they reached for something they thought they should say rather than digging into their deep seated internal beliefs. The fundamental problem with the above list is that it's not personal to any particular company, it's what most come up with when pushed, so it's not helping them differentiate themselves from competitors. I'm pretty sure I've shared some views on that!

A lot of businesses, through their marketing, tend to concentrate on telling their customers WHAT they do. A car company tends to tell their customer they sell cars, a coffee shop tends to tell their customers they sell coffee. *"What's wrong with that?"*, you may ask.

Well, in a crowded market, it becomes increasingly hard to differentiate one company from another if all you are shown are the products. As a customer, you already know what you want and you already know what the company sells, so you need more tangibles to further differentiate one company from another.

Strong brands concentrate on WHY they are in business, then they look at HOW they can provide the product or service and finally will consider WHAT they do. Pretty much the opposite of what start-ups and SMEs tend to do. Hence me continuing to write and share.

This final building block, which is quite lengthy compared to the rest, is an approach I'm urging entrepreneurs like you to take - if you want to "build a brand" rather than simply "grow a business".

Valunify

Luckily for you, I have devised my own system to help business owners identify their own values. The system can also be extended to identify the values of the current employees and whether this is aligned with the culture of the business or indeed at odds with it. With my Valunify process we can "tap and map" the individuals' values by producing a set of charts. These illustrate where shared values within a business may overlap to help suggest some core messages. These are then far more powerful than the basic prerequisites of business that continue to show up in the aforementioned top ten list.

Similar in principle to D.I.S.C. profiling or a Myers-Briggs personality assessment, the Valunify process will uncover certain aspects of your value system that you may not be able to articulate when put on the spot. But after a session you will certainly say, "*Yep, that makes sense!*".

A great differentiating element of a business to buy INTO is its beliefs, its philosophy, its values and culture. A shared sense of passion and a clear set of values hailing from the company's leaders down through the business becomes powerfully unifying for both employees, contractors, suppliers and customers alike. Once you can establish an authentic foundation of passions, values and attitudes, we can evolve and consistently relay core messages through all interactions to a customer, be that via marketing collateral, face-to-face meetings, on phones or through social and advertising media.

Charting a course

I'll share the results of a Valunify exercise I carried out with an I.T. business, so you can see how the information is mapped out. I hope you understand that I can't fully show the "magic" ingredient that converts the data into the results as that's my highly valuable IP. But you can certainly buy it off my website!! The original names of the employees and the business have been taken off to protect their identities.

The prerequisite chart

The first chart above maps out the top 10 most repeated "values" when asking a business *"What do they stand for?"*.

The spread across the chart is pretty even, so doesn't really highlight a strong direction to tap into. As an aside, if you can't deliver on these values or promises, then in most cases, you shouldn't really be in business!

Because these charts are geared towards an individual's value system, it won't mean that a company will necessarily "grow", for instance, if the top half is shaded. It would suggest that a majority of individuals feel it's important that they are given the opportunity to grow, in the broadest sense.

Firstly we looked for the boss's top ten values, and through the process we find that they are:

Reputation

Excitement

Success

Ambitious

Wealth

Principled

Loyalty

Intelligence

Humour

Fun

———

These values are then mapped out like so:

First thing to notice is that there are different values to choose from, other than the usual suspects! In fact, the process offers the individual 120 to choose from. The next thing is to notice what the mapping is telling us. Not too unexpected for a boss, I would suggest: pushing towards achievement which would be a good trait for someone in charge of a company. Not a fan of being power hungry, that's good!

Firmly values personal direction and is tangibly close to having an understanding of the pros of being open to change. We can then see a sprinkling of other values, but nothing at all pulling in an opposite direction.

Here are some of the employees:

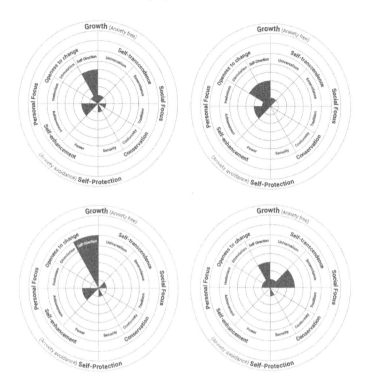

Then the results are mapped on top of each other to see where the most overlapping or shared values are:

Interestingly, the employees tended to peak collectively with "self-direction" and "benevolence", with employee number four having the majority of their values in "self-direction". That particular employee handed their notice in three months later! To me, this came as no shock considering how much that employee valued self-direction. They went off and literally did their own thing!

The process can be helpful when trying to understand internal relationships, dynamics, motivations and rewards. These results don't completely highlight other traits within individuals, like behavioural styles, which are a combination of inherent and learned skills. However, if the individuals were completely honest with themselves, then this exercise highlights a person's deep rooted values which are pretty unwavering. We must say that, like behavioural styles, we can all possess a variety of values that need to reflect many varied characteristics. However, with the luxury of this process you can graphically see an individual's inherent preference for personal growth or social recognition, for instance. In a lot of cases, that's something that even the individual would find difficult to articulate.

With this insight, we can observe four specific results which can also help in the understanding of the company's culture, what it stands for and how its brand values can be harnessed.

1. The leader's values.
2. The employees' values.
3. Leadership vs employee values.
4. Breakdown of individuals' value words.

More importantly, you may start to understand how a company can best attract customers who share the same values; customers who will buy INTO the company's philosophies, beliefs and culture as well as its products and services. The results can then inform company core messaging which can be promoted through marketing strategies and can also help with recruiting like-minded individuals.

Ultimately, we see that this process gives you a new understanding to discover where there are strengths and opportunities in your business that you may not have known about before. When I've used this tool, it has clearly helped us focus on developing an authentic value based set of messages for brand and marketing strategies for our clients. More notably, it helps with developing the promise to the customer which we can then reflect with internal mantras and external straplines. This is an extra special chapter all by itself... coming up next!

VALUE - STRATEGY QUESTIONS

1. How have you protected your business / offer / service / product against competition? Not just through trademarking, there are all sorts of intellectual property you can protect as well.

2. What is in place to allow your business / offer / service / product to operate without you? Another thing you might forget to protect is YOURSELF. This is more about getting proper shareholders' agreements in place and other insurances.

3. What is your plan to sell your business / offer / service / product for the highest possible value?

A LICK OF PAINT

Let's Get Engaged
Tools Down

LET'S GET ENGAGED

AN EMOTIONAL STRAPLINE

You may have jumped here from the "promise" or "original" chapter as I did stress how much I feel that a strapline can be enormously helpful for a business culture and for customer engagement. So, I'll expand on what I mean by that.

It's the last tool in the "holy trinity" towards graphically representing your business offer. No hard and fast rules as usual, so I'm not going to tell you what's right and what's wrong here, but we should explore my usual observations between the big brands and the start-ups who might be missing a trick or two.

Let's make sure we understand each other first. A strapline or tagline or memory hook is the three to six words that the voiceover artist says at the end of the advert as it swipes from left to right across the screen.

"I'm lovin' it",
"Every little helps",
"It does exactly what it says on the tin".

Hopefully you may recognise them and you may know which company or product they are associated with. Then again you may not, and not because they don't work but perhaps you are not their audience.

In the form of a quiz, I've presented such straplines in talks and most recognise about two out of three. Ronseal's "*It does exactly what it says on the tin*" sometimes gets attributed to Cuprinol. Whoops! However, a lot of people will quote that strapline about any other product that suggests that its promise is very much "to the point". It has become part of our society's everyday language, which I'm sure Ronseal are happy about, even if one in three people think they are quoting their competitor!

There are plenty of companies that don't have straplines and you may well know some that don't. Of course one conclusion when seeing a successful business without one is to suggest you don't need one. The BBC, for instance, doesn't have one. After many years of trading, it now chooses to use my arch enemy - an acronym - for a name. And it doesn't even have a proper logo for that matter! (I'm not "dissing" Martin Lambie-Nairn's design, there are good strong reasons for the current logo based on many factors, do read up on Wikipedia!). Unfortunately for the purpose of this book, it goes against everything I'm writing about and there's one other really good reason for that. The BBC is part of the woven fabric of practically everybody in British society and many parts of the globe. When your business is that successful, hey, chuck this book away and do what you want, you've made it! Until then, can I urge you to read on a bit more?

I'm not here to argue that you NEED a strapline, I'm just aware that they can be extremely useful. I've even seen ones I have come up with completely change the culture of a business - for the good, that is! The last building block chapter about finding your company values has often led me to then start developing a strapline for a company.

I wish I had ten reasons to have a strapline, cos everyone loves a top ten. But I do have eight!

1. Your business name and the logo may not have told the whole story of your differentiating offer or proposition yet.
2. There's a chance to get another core message or two in front of your audience.
3. It also offers a chance to emotionally engage your audience and show off some personality.
4. A "good" strapline will undoubtedly differentiate you from your competition.
5. You can register a strapline as a trademark which increases the value of your business.
6. It would be cool if it resonates so well that society started using it in other ways (even if they thought you were someone else!).
7. It will focus and inform your working process to stay on track with your promise.
8. It can unify and focus your staff to also buy into the reason you are in business, especially when it taps into shared values.

They already know what you do!

So where do we start to create a strapline? Well, first I must urge you not to do the obvious and simply tell your audience what you do... a little counter intuitive you might think? As with my initial premise of starting with WHY you are in business, your customer already knows WHAT you do. So don't waste that message on them, give them something else to latch on to. Most SMEs fall into this trap almost every time and you will notice that established brands tend not to. It's a panic move and doesn't help differentiate you from your competition, here's what happens.

You could start with describing your business offer in 30 words for instance, yes way too long for a strapline but you might get some nuggets eventually if you whittle it down. Here's a process for Sainsbury's, for instance:

> *"A modern and innovative multinational retailer providing a comprehensive range of in-store and online grocery and general merchandise products and services built around our customers, our colleagues and their communities."*

Let's try 20 words, should be easy to just trim the fat.

> *"A modern and innovative multinational retailer providing a range of in-store and online grocery and general merchandise products and services."*

Ten words, we're really going to have to cut out some useful stuff, but should be left with what is important.

> *"An in-store and online multinational grocery and general merchandise retailer."*

Maybe six words? This is getting harder, but also very therapeutic!

> *"Multinational grocery and general merchandise retailer."*

O.K. let's go for broke, three words should absolutely define what we're about!

> *"Multinational grocery retailer."*

Et voilà, you've summed up exactly what Sainsbury's offer as a business. Unfortunately you have also unveiled exactly what Tesco, Morrisons and Asda do as well. By adding a strapline that tells your customers exactly what you and your competition do, you have not informed them of anything that they didn't know already. This is another reminder to show us that looking at what big brands do can really help a start-up. It's not two different worlds. You operate in the same world, the world where you need to connect with your customer more than your competitor does, "simples"!

The whittling down of the "Sainsbury's proposition" exercise hopefully shows you that it's not the preferred route for big brands. The actual strapline for each of the aforementioned supermarkets are:

Sainsbury's
"Live well for less"
(used to be: *Eat well for less*)
Tesco
"Every little helps"
Morrisons
"Makes it"
(used to be: *More of what matters*),
Asda
"Save money, live better"
(used to be: *Saving you money every day*).

We have to recognise that you and I are probably consumers of these brands already, and we know them very well. So to tell you that you sub-consciously buy from Sainsbury's above Morrisons because you were more persuaded by the strapline is going to be hard for you to swallow. It may very well be because you live closer. My point at this stage of your brand development is that no one knows you exist at all and, dare I say it, "every little helps" when reaching out to your customer and differentiating you from your competition.

Using the above examples should show you that the different straplines push different messages. Tesco is pushing customer service, but in such a way that there is no real commitment or promise, just to try and do as little as they can (I jest!). Joking aside, this kind of strapline or "promise" is hard not to deliver on, so it's very safe. Sainsbury's themselves are pushing a "quality product" and "competitive pricing", which they have done for decades. Their customers used to be able to simply "*Eat well for less*" but now it's a whole "lifestyle" promise with the introduction of "*Live well...*". Recent years have brought the customer a "brand match" campaign, so almost suggesting there's no point shopping anywhere else cos they will match the price, almost eliminating the need to compete. "Almost" being the operative word, because as we should know by now, branding is about being able to charge a higher price as long as you offer value in return. Morrisons have recently changed their strapline to "*Makes it*" which has to be said in conjunction with the word Morrisons, as it becomes a continuation of a sentence. It's gone a bit more lifestyle again, which is an attempt at re-positioning themselves in the market. It could be read as "Makes your tea" or "Makes your day". Again the ambiguity at this level makes it easy to deliver on a very low level promise. Nonetheless, it's different from the previous two. Asda however is just plain being naughty! "*Save money, live better*" is exactly the same as Sainsbury's where their priority is price over lifestyle. Bang goes my argument for using a strapline to be original or even different! Asda are being the same in a different way.

Anyway, the whole point of all that is to underline that they don't all say "*Multinational grocery retailer*" they try (except Asda!) to give you another message or benefit or market positioning clue (like price). The supermarkets are quite tame in their approach and perhaps don't push personality, possibly because it is such a cut-throat market. Your strapline could suggest an emotional concept like Sky's "*Believe in better*", an instructional engagement like Subway's "*Eat fresh*", a performance claim like BMW's *"The ultimate driving machine"*. If you really think no one will get what you do unless you make it as clear as possible, try Npower's *"Electric and Gas"*!

Reason seven for a strapline was that it will "focus and inform your working process". Let's take Red Bull's wacky *"Gives you wings"*. From my perspective as a branding consultant I rather enjoyed the strapline and was happy to see a company being different, pushing a boundary to see how far they could take it. The product was an intensely caffeinated soft drink that may well "perk you up", but the strapline pushed that concept a bit further. The company itself became synonymous with sponsoring extreme sports where most of the competitors "flew" whether in an actual plane, diving off a cliff or doing a somersault on a motorbike. The brand alignment was spot on. Their adverts for some reason were very different in style and not extreme but the cartoon characters would all end up drinking a can of Red Bull, sprout wings and start flying. The strapline absolutely informed the marketing decisions:

"Does this sport we're thinking of sponsoring 'give you wings?'"

"YES"

"Let's sponsor it then!"

Red Bull's target audience got it, but unfortunately, as noted earlier, it just takes one idiot to make it all go sour as one person sued Red Bull for false advertising claiming that their product did not provide them with wings. They settled out of court. Hey, let's not be fearful of being different. Much like the music industry of late, you'll notice it's only people or businesses with squillions of pounds who get sued, cos there's more chance of getting some money.

You are a small business, so that's not going to happen. But just to make absolutely sure, let's not claim anything too outrageous that you can't deliver on.

On the subject of the soft drinks market, you may have heard of Coca-Cola! I mention this company and their products because it shows that a strapline isn't for life, and sometimes it can be just for Christmas. Coca-Cola or Coke has had around 60 different straplines in conjunction with their top selling product; many more if you include other English-speaking regions with different cultures, and then more on top of that when including the rest of the world. One strapline may spring to mind depending on when you first interacted with the product, much like a life changing album usually heard when in your formative teenage years. Mine was "*It's the real thing*" which lasted from 1969 to 1975. Another one that stuck with me was "*Coke is it*". I think both connected with me because of the songs or jingles that accompanied them, as I am very much a muso as well. "*I'd like to buy the world a coke*" was the song especially co-written with Bristol's all-time great songwriters, Roger Cook and Roger Greenaway for the advert at the time which included the strapline "*It's the real thing*". Due to popular demand for the commercial to be played on radio as if it was a "proper song", The New Seekers, who sang that original, later recorded another version called "*I'd like to teach the world to sing*". A powerful strapline that again informed and focused a strong campaign and period of marketing for Coca-Cola.

A change in company strapline might be as subtle as something to use as a headline for an advertising campaign or new product launch. So the original strapline may come back into play. You may have thought Sainsbury's strapline was "*Taste the difference*", but that is more of a campaign slogan for a range of foods that still come under the overall company strapline of "*Live well for less*". A bigger reason for noticing a change in a strapline can be because of a change within a market beyond a company's control. So you may have to change direction or diversify to survive. With a change of direction your internal strategies may have to change. Or even internal values or promises may have to change, and you should therefore reflect that in your messaging to your customer. Of course, that could also be reflected in your name and logo. But I stick with the link between internal strategy and an external strapline, as I feel they are more closely linked when communicating your promise to your customer.

Guy Kawasaki is someone to look up and read about, where he shares his views on company "mantras" as he calls them. In my view, and I think in his, a mantra is much stronger than a strapline. It is more of an internal company belief, rather than an external message to your customer. Mr Kawasaki basically suggests to stop "peeing about" with a lengthy mission statement, and get to the crux of your passion, promise, belief or indeed mission and try to do it in three words - much like our earlier exercise. In this case, the exercise is not to narrow down WHAT you do, but to hone in on WHY you are in business in the first place, the HOW you are going to change the world and WHAT do you stand for. I think I may have referenced that before!

Let's take Nike for instance. Again, when I've held a quiz during a talk most people recognise their strapline as "*Just do it*". The standard one in three people quizzed think it belongs to B&Q because that's so close to "*You can do it*". Never mind! It is a strong "instructional" no holds barred strapline, even stronger than Apple's "*Think different*" or Evian's "*Live young*". But it is somewhat different from the company's internal mantra or heavily summarised mission statement, which is "*Authentic athletic performance*". Most business owners will understand that an internal mission statement would ordinarily help towards decision making, strategy planning, focusing on where to go next... When it's captured in just three words then everyone can understand it, there's no confusion. Some internal mantras may well become the external strapline, but a consumer sometimes needs something else to capture their imagination as they are not working for you. Yes, you want them to buy into your passion and share your outlook on life, but they may need a different connection, a different encouragement. The Nike way to encourage their customers is to say *"Just do it"*. Along with the associated advertising campaigns, it broadens to imply other encouragements like: *"Never give up"*, *"You can do it"*; no matter who you are or your background, work hard and anything is possible. All of which is far more effective than exclaiming the phrase *"Authentic athletic performance"*. Their internal mantra informs everyone in the company why they are in business and what they strive for on a daily basis. You couldn't keep telling your staff to *"Just do it"*!

Apples and pears mate

I'll end this section, and the entire book, with a story of a strapline I came up with for a local fruit and vegetable wholesaler who at the time were called A.David and Co Ltd, which we later re-branded to Arthur David. We had basically been their outsourced design agency for many years, and I had always wanted to re-brand them and change their logo but it didn't happen. Partly, I suspected, for fear of change and most significantly it would cost a lot of money to change all the van livery! Then one day, possibly ten years on, the two directors I dealt with invited me along to a meeting which centred around a possible change of strapline. Still no new logo yet! The meeting went on for a couple of hours and it simply centred around me asking: *"WHY are you in business?"* and *"WHAT are you passionate about?"*. As you now know, sometimes these questions can bring up very dull obvious answers: excellent customer service, the best quality products, all the prerequisites for business as described in the values chapter. I knew that these guys worked extremely hard, so I just got them talking, as I normally do. I shut up, listened and wrote stuff down. Sometimes, after 25 years of doing my job, this may be all the time I need to instinctively know what's needed. Looking at my notes after about two hours of listening, I had circled the phrase *"Leave it with us"*. The two directors had uttered this phrase countless times in different guises, *"Let me get back to you."*, *"Leave it with me and I'll call later."* etc. They had been describing their telesales enquiry process and, unbeknownst to them, had identified the very thing that differentiated them from their competition.

The players in their market, like most markets, produced brochures and websites showing their products. The understood reaction from a competitor with an enquiry from a customer was that "If it's not in the brochure then we haven't got it."! This was not Arthur David's approach. Actually it wasn't even a calculated approach, it was simply part of their passion. It didn't matter if a product wasn't in the brochure; or if they had never heard of a rare herb grown on the highest rock face in Outer Mongolia that a customer was desperate for. They would just say, *"Leave it with me; I'll see what I can find and get back to you."* or a version of that.

For me this was going to be the meeting where our relationship might reach a turning point. In nine cases out of ten, a small business doesn't want to take a risk with a strapline that looks "mysterious". They would prefer *"Selling quality fruit and veg to the South West"*. Hopefully, after this chapter you can appreciate that type of strapline is meaningless. So, with a huge intake of breath I showed them what I had circled and said,

"Leave it with us" really should be your strapline, because fundamentally after listening to you for two hours it is quite

clearly your internal mantra as well, even if you weren't aware of it. In most cases an agency would go away and perhaps do lots of "research" to justify the charges, but I was pretty sure this was the time to be bold. I'm not going to suggest it was an epiphany moment for the directors, it was more, "*that's interesting*", and of course I put my arguments forward for being brave enough to think like big brands think. I had also brought along a proposal to change the logo and name of the business, but figured that would be pushing my luck!

As a quick aside, I'd like to point out a lesson in value and worth here, which might be useful. It may seem like it took me two hours to come up with that strapline. At the time, it actually took me 20 years and two hours.

Moving on...

It's all very well tapping into the owner's passion, of course that's where it starts. The ultimate goal is to get the staff to buy into that passion (mantra), because it's your staff that interact with your customers - in their case, every minute of every day. Sometimes I'm asked to deliver branding strategies and rationale to the staff; so it doesn't look like the bosses are just laying down the law yet again. In this case, the directors would lead the delivery of the strategy and explain to the staff why the company's new strapline was going to have the power to focus everything they would do from now on.

It worked.

With a decent rationale behind the strapline and more importantly, authenticity, the staff totally bought into it. They proceeded to ask for a huge banner to be put on the wall of the telesales office and get it placed on all the screen savers. Then, in an act of complete madness or complete passionate belief to the cause, one of the directors had "my" strapline tattooed on his arm to show his commitment!

They also agreed to a new logo!

TOOLS DOWN
AN ACKNOWLEDGED GOODBYE

Well, I think that's it. I'm outta gas, depleted and spent.

If there is any more wisdom in me that can be imparted it's well and truly buried, forgotten or not relevant!

If you just take one thing away from this read, then it's been worth the past five years of typing. If there's a couple more nuggets you can implement or try out, then hopefully it will change the course of your venture for the better.

As I write this very sentence I know I'll firstly be handing the book over to my editor to change all the grammar and spelling mistakes. Then I'll be asking some of my clients to give it a read to prompt some glowing testimonials for future marketing!

Three weeks later...

I'd now like to say how deeply humbled I am by those wonderful comments and kind words from the clients I carefully chose to put on the back on the book!

I am of course genuinely grateful to everyone who has supported and trusted me, my advice and the business I run alongside my wonderful wife Mandy.

An enormous debt of gratitude goes to Huw Bendon of On Point Copywriting who edited this book and has been my go to copywriter for many years.

Finally, it would be remiss of me to not add a "call to action". So if you do want to reach out for more help on a one-to-one basis, or to ask me to talk to a group of fresh entrepreneurs, then please do get in touch. Hopefully this book demonstrates my WHY, which is: to help, and to witness, businesses like yours to flourish.

Now go build a brand!

———

The Flint Website
https://www.theflint.co.uk

Bits'n'blogs
https://www.brandgrenade.co.uk

from bland to **BRAND**

written by Jason Flinter

Printed in Great Britain
by Amazon

77386036R00122